A Child Is Not A Toy

A Child Is Not A Toy

Voices of Children in Poverty

Sheila Baxter

New Star Books Ltd. ❖ Vancouver ❖ 1993

Printed and bound in Canada by Best-Gagné Book Manufacturers
1 2 3 4 5 97 96 95 94 93
First Printing, April 1993

Published by
New Star Books Ltd.
2504 York Avenue
Vancouver, B.C.
V6K 1E3

Editor: Audrey McClellan
Index: Teresa Murphy
Cover design: Gek-Bee Siow

The publisher is grateful for assistance provided by the Canada Council, the Department of Communications Book Publishing Industry Development Program, and the Cultural Services Branch, Province of British Columbia

Canadian Cataloguing in Publication Data

Baxter, Sheila, 1933-
A child is not a toy

Includes bibliographical references and index.
ISBN 0-921586-26-4
1. Poor children—British Columbia. 2. Poor children—British Columbia—Case studies. I. Title
HV745.B7B39 1993362.7'08'6C93-091261-6

Contents

Tables

Dedicated to my grandchildren

Notes to Readers

When I interviewed children who were poor, I always phrased the questions in a way that would not embarrass or hurt them. For instance, I wouldn't say "You are poor. How do you feel?" Instead, I would ask "How do children that are poor feel? How do children that are poor feel in school?" As a result, the answers from the children are mostly phrased in the second person, referring to "you" not "I." Using second person seemed to make it easier for children to express their own feelings. The adults who were poor as children speak of their painful memories mostly in the first person, as "I."

Some children gave me drawings instead of interviews. These sketches tell as much about poverty and its effects on children as the interviews do. Sometimes children wrote their own explanation; others, who were too young or unable to write, told an adult what the sketch was about, and the adult faithfully recorded the answer. Some of the sketches will be easy to print but some won't. The quality of the print is not the issue; it's the world as the child sees it that is the message.

The children and adults I interviewed are from many cultures and ethnic backgrounds. The common denominator is poverty, although there are a couple of interviews and sketches from children living above the poverty line. All names have been changed to protect the people I've interviewed. If a child has an anglo-sounding name, it doesn't necessarily mean he or she is an anglophone or a WASP. A high percentage of my interviews were with people of colour. I don't specify a person's colour, race, sexual orientation, or other details unless they are mentioned in the interview.

I have tried to reinforce what the children say by interviewing people who work with children, who can give further examples and explain the system that causes, or solves, some of the problems. The interviews with social workers and advocates are not intended to "prove" what the children say is true. Children don't need adults to validate what they tell me. They speak the truth. It is so obvious that these children have to be heard.

What is the Poverty Line?

There are various formulas and statistics used to determine the poverty line, but Statistics Canada defines the "low income cut-off" (LICO) as an income level at which families spend 20 percent more of their income than the average family on food, shelter, and clothing. The National Council of Welfare, in its publication *Poverty Profile, 1980-1990*, says, "The average Canadian family spent 36.2 percent of gross income on food, shelter, and clothing according to the most recent data on spending patterns, so it was assumed that low-income Canadians spent 56.2 percent or more on the necessities of life." (As the following tables show, though, many families are living far below that line.) LICOs are revised periodically as the cost of living changes, and different studies use different age definitions and statistics from different years. The Yukon and Northwest Territories are not included in the survey which determines the LICOs. I've tried to avoid using lots of stats; it will be obvious that the people I talk to and hear about do not have enough money for all their needs. Whether they are 10 or 50 percent below an arbitrary poverty line, there is no doubt they are living in poverty.

NATIONAL COUNCIL OF WELFARE ESTIMATES OF STATISTICS CANADA'S LOW INCOME CUT-OFFS (1986 BASE) FOR 1992

	Community Size				
Family Size	*500,000+*	*100,000-499,999*	*30,000-99,999*	*less than 30,000*	*rural*
1	$15,426	$13,549	$13,237	$12,066	$10,502
2	$20,910	$18,367	$17,942	$16,356	$14,237
3	$26,579	$23,344	$22,805	$20,789	$18,096
4	$30,548	$26,876	$26,357	$23,936	$20,834
5	$33,435	$29,366	$28,688	$26,152	$22,762
6	$36,293	$31,874	$31,139	$28,386	$24,708
7+	$39,034	$34,285	$33,494	$30,533	$26,575

Source: National Council of Welfare

COMPARISON OF MINIMUM WAGE INCOME TO POVERTY LINE INCOME FOR ONE PARENT WITH ONE CHILD, 1990

Jurisdiction	*Minimum wage*	*Annual minimum wage income*	*Poverty line*	*Income as % of poverty line*
Canada	$4.00	$7,904	$19,200	41.2
Nfld.	$4.25	$8,398	$16,900	49.7
P.E.I.	$4.50	$8,892	$15,000	59.3
N.S.	$4.50	$8,892	$16,900	52.6
N.B.	$4.50	$8,892	$16,900	52.6
Quebec	$5.00	$9,880	$19,200	51.5
Ontario	$5.00	$9,880	$19,200	51.5
Manitoba	$4.70	$9,287	$19,200	48.4
Sask.	$4.75	$9,386	$16,900	55.5
Alberta	$4.50	$8,892	$19,200	46.3
B.C.	$5.00	$9,880	$19,200	51.5

Note: Minimum wages are those prevailing on April 1, 1990. Minimum wage income is based on a 38-hour work week, and 52 weeks of work. The poverty line is the estimated Statistics Canada low income cut-off for each province's largest city.

Source: Standing Senate Committee on Social Affairs, Science and Technology, *Children in Poverty: Toward a Better Future.*

ADEQUACY OF BENEFITS, 1991

Province	*Family Size*	*Total income*	*LICO*	*Total income as % of LICO*
Nfld.	1 parent, 1 child	$12,347	$17,802	69
	Couple, 2 children	$14,561	$26,049	56
P.E.I.	1 parent, 1 child	$12,343	$17,290	71
	Couple, 2 children	$18,698	$25,449	73
N.S.	1 parent, 1 child	$11,961	$17,802	67
	Couple, 2 children	$15,065	$26,049	58
N.B.	1 parent, 1 child	$9,841	$17,802	55
	Couple, 2 children	$11,721	$26,049	45
Quebec	1 parent, 1 child	$10,975	$20,266	54
	Couple, 2 children	$15,426	$29,661	52
Ontario	1 parent, 1 child	$16,098	$20,266	79
	Couple, 2 children	$21,472	$29,661	72
Manitoba	1 parent, 1 child	$11,167	$20,266	55
	Couple, 2 children	$19,812	$29,661	67
Sask.	1 parent, 1 child	$12,028	$17,802	68
	Couple, 2 children	$17,059	$26,049	65

Alberta	1 parent, 1 child	$11,630	$20,266	57
	Couple, 2 children	$18,365	$29,661	62
B.C.	1 parent, 1 child	$12,478	$20,266	62
	Couple, 2 children	$16,134	$29,661	54

Source: National Council of Welfare, *Welfare Incomes 1991.*

Journal

It is May 1992. I have been avoiding writing this book, but it has never left my mind. There is always a small voice saying, "What about the children? Who is listening to them?" In my last two books, adult voices were heard speaking out against poverty and homelessness. Now it's the children's turn.

For the next nine months I will try to give children a voice. I will interview children who live below the poverty line, and perhaps a couple of children who are not poor, to see how they relate to children who are poor. (How I hate this word "poor"; the very sound of it is so demoralizing.)

I look back, remembering the fifteen-year-old girl I interviewed in my last book, living in a run-down hotel with her family. I wonder, did she survive?

I was at a local community centre, having a cheap lunch. Two young girls came in. They said they were hungry. One, a small person about fifteen, looked really nervous and scared. The other I had met before. She had been homeless then. We talked. The two girls had been living in an empty house. The young people squatting in the house had been busted by the police. The older girl was trying to talk the younger into going to Toronto. The younger girl turned to me nervously and said, "I have spots. I'm really itchy." I looked at the spots and said, "Honey, you've got scabies." She said, "The mattress I slept on was really dirty." I talked to her about where she could go for help, and the older girl said she would take her to the youth clinic. After they ate, they took off real fast. They obviously didn't want to be picked up and questioned by any authority. In B.C. you are not an adult until you are nineteen, and till then, you can be picked up and returned to your family, or put in foster care. These two were scared of being taken back to wherever they had run from. They lived scrounging, panhandling. They were street kids, hungry street kids.

I called Betty McPhee at Crabtree Corners. They have a daycare for children and a drop-in for street people. I asked her how she felt about me writing this book. She said, "It's wonderful. It just gives me goose bumps." Then I talked to Jean Swanson and Linda Marcotte at End Legislated Poverty and asked them for ideas. Linda said, "Perhaps you should make some rules for interviewing children." We agreed that it was something that had to be handled with great care.

When I talk to parents about the possibility of interviewing their children, I become even more aware of how gently I must tread. This is the most sensitive issue I have ever dealt with. I asked different anti-poverty activists and people who work with children how I could address the issue of poverty. I obviously can't say to a child, "Are you poor? What does it feel like?" I know that the self esteem of children is often very fragile. I ask at what age does a child know that he or she is poor. Most say it starts in the school.

Flashing back to my poverty as a child, I have memories of deep shame, intense hunger, of begging for money, daydreaming about being adopted and having nice clothes and shoes, about going to school and having the children like and accept me. That didn't happen, and if it had, I wouldn't be the anti-poverty activist I am today.

I have given a lot of thought to what rules I should give myself when interviewing children. I decided on the following.

- They don't have to talk to me if they don't want to.
- No one will know who they are unless they choose to identify themselves.
- They don't have to answer any questions that they choose not to.

- Their interviews will be played back to them.
- A parent can be with them if they wish.
- I will believe what they tell me.

Chris, the coordinator of the Downtown Eastside Women's Centre, came across very strong on one point. She told me that I shouldn't label women as single mothers. As soon as someone reads the phrase "single mothers," all kinds of judgments and prejudices spring up, and society dumps the problem on the fact that there is a "single mother" involved. She is right, so in this book I will say "family." That can mean one or two people of any sex, or even an extended family. One woman I spoke to talked about her street brother and sister, her street mother and father.

As I speak to families who live below the poverty line, I realize that having their children talk about their poverty is really difficult for parents. Many go out of their way to hide it from their children. One parent told of a ten-year-old daughter who badly needed a pair of shoes. The daughter said, "I need shoes. How am I going to get them?" She wasn't asking her parent for the shoes, she was taking the responsibility as if she were an adult. I asked if I could interview the girl. Her parent said, "I'll think about it and I'll ask her."

A friend called me. She knew a family whose children are very artistic. She had asked if one of the children could do a drawing about poverty. She couldn't understand why the parent she asked got mad and said no. I understand. Poverty creates a terrible guilt feeling when you are a parent and you can't get your children the things they need.

My eldest son, now married with a family, is middle class as far as income goes. He said, "You know, Mom, the first time I knew we were poor was when the Baptist Church brought us a charity basket at Christmas." My husband was a low-paid blue-collar worker at the time. I remember the incident. It was a snowy cold Québec winter. We lived in a third-floor walk-up flat. Laundry was done in a wringer washer, and a clothesline was strung along the hall to dry the clothes, because they froze when hung outside in the winter, and of course I didn't have a dryer. As they came into the hall, those church people looked at the laundry and I'm sure they judged us by it. Anyway, John was about ten years of age. He became enraged. He said, "We don't need your charity, we are not poor. Give it to somebody else." I remember hushing him. How he hated that moment when he first became aware that we were poor. It still bothers him, I think.

❖

I ran into a friend on the street. It was a really nice sunny day. Spring in Vancouver is so beautiful. The flowers were in bloom, masses of reds and yellows and all kinds of colours – a joy to look at. I asked my friend, "What's happening?" She told me they couldn't afford a babysitter and a new friend of the family had volunteered to look after the children. The friend started to buy the daughter all kinds of clothes that the family couldn't afford. Now, two years later, the thirteen-year-old girl is a runaway and sexually active because this so-called friendly babysitter had been sexually abusing her and keeping her quiet by buying her stuff. My friend said, "He set my daughter up for prostitution. If I hadn't been poor and working an under-the-table job, I would not have been so desperate for a sitter." The daughter was missing. The family had tried to get help, but the girl just kept running away. After we parted, the spring flowers seemed less bright, even invisible.

I can't just switch off and on I guess. This is so frustrating. Poverty is a catch-22: you need to work but you can't afford a sitter, so if someone offers to sit for free, you accept, even though the person may be a threat to your children, a predator. Poverty can set kids up for sexual abuse.

❖

Way back in 1959 the United Nations drafted a declaration on the rights of the child. Paragraph 4 says:

> The child shall enjoy the benefits of social security. He shall be entitled to grow and develop in health; to this end, special care and protection shall be provided to him and his mother, including adequate pre-natal and post-natal care. The child shall have the right to adequate nutrition, housing, recreation, and medical services.

Thirty-odd years ago this was declared and yet in our affluent country we still have children living far below the poverty level. We have homeless children. Recently, the federal government cut back on social housing, even though the waiting lists are endless.

In November 1989, the Canadian parliament passed a resolution with the goal of eliminating poverty among Canadian children by the year 2000. A *Globe and Mail* article from November 1991 says that progress is not evident. Apparently the government established a children's bureau in the Health and Welfare Department to coordinate the anti-poverty campaign. The children's bureau has a budget of almost $2 million, and is run by Brian Ward, a former aide to Prime Minister Brian Mulroney, but it is not able to deliver any programs. In fact, it can't really do much because policy is controlled by the finance minister's office, and that office is more concerned about the recession than about social policy. I guess a lot of people earned a lot of money doing all these studies and reports, but wouldn't it be great if part of their salary depended on results, like sales people working on commission?

It's been my experience in the last twenty years of anti-poverty work that millions and millions of dollars go for studies that are supposed to find solutions to poverty. *Yet children are still not guaranteed good housing, good food, and good schools.*

Today my editor and publisher, Audrey and Rolf, came to see me. They looked over the proposal for this book and obviously supported it. I agreed to have it done by the end of the year. Then maybe it will be a spring book. They came bearing gifts: Audrey loaned me a typewriter that was decent and Rolf brought paper, files, and a notebook. I don't apply for Canada Council grants for my books, so the gifts really help. The benefit of working with a small publishing company is empowerment – it's like working with good, honest friends. None of us are rich, there's no classism. Instead, there's a gentle discussion of ideas and there's a feeling, for me, of trust that goes both ways. Having a publisher and editor who believe in my work is a must!

I had some disturbing news today, as well. A parent that I interviewed in my last book called me. The family had spent a lot of time in shelters because, at the time, it was very difficult to find affordable rentals on a welfare budget. One of the children is now a street kid; another is in foster care. How can children survive the trauma of being in a shelter? of being homeless?

❖

As I talk to parents and workers, I am told that some children not only are poor but have been sexually abused too. That doesn't mean that because parents are poor they will sexually abuse their children. Rich and middle-class children are sexually abused too, but I think poor children are more at risk from outside sources because of non-safe housing, poor recreation resources, unscreened helpers who turn out to be pedophiles. Pedophiles buy children toys and clothes that families can't supply them with, and then sexually abuse them. Street kids are picked up and given drugs and money by johns who want to have sex with children. I realize that even though this is a book about children and poverty, sexual abuse will probably show up in some of the sketches and interviews.

❖

As a society, do we love our children? The evidence is to the contrary. It's not so long ago that our children worked in the mines and industry from dusk to dawn. At one time, children were deliberately maimed so they could legally beg. According to Statistics Canada, in 1991 there were 1.2 million children living in poverty in Canada. This number is rapidly increasing.

Many single people, seniors, and couples without children (not all of them!) complain about other peoples' children. I have heard them say, "We didn't give birth to them; it's up to their parents to support them. They shouldn't have children if they can't support them." Many resent paying school taxes, or seeing their tax money go to child benefit payments or to fund daycare.

When I visited the Okanagan recently, I saw blocks and blocks of complexes surrounded by strong walls. Adult Only Complexes, the signs said, Adult, Adult, Adult, and more and more were being built. It was like the olden days, when forts were built and castles had moats. The family I was with had three children. They said, "You kinda get the feeling that kids are not welcome." Or even liked.

In the year 2021 there will be more than 6 million people in Canada over the age of 65 – one in every four Canadians will be a senior, and it is the children growing up now who will have the job of looking after us. They will be the doctors, nurses, homemakers, cooks, dentists, caregivers. So isn't it in society's best interest to take care of and nurture our children? If we set an example by being unloving and uncaring about their poverty, how do we expect them to treat us when we need them? They will have to pay the taxes to support medicare, and to keep social housing and long-term care facilities open. If we don't nourish and educate them, there will be huge numbers of unemployed and no money for medicare and pensions.

Roberta Baxter

❖

I have found some really neat people as I gather my research, and many of them give me helpful ideas. Rosemary, at the National Anti-Poverty Organization in Ottawa, suggested I look into child labour. She also sent me up-to-date, relevant material. The Ombudsman's office in Victoria sent me some reports that had been published, and some statistics for B.C. It's so important that I have up-to-date stats and information that pertain to child poverty and abuse, and I depend on a network of "good people" who are involved in the anti-poverty movement.

The people at End Legislated Poverty in Vancouver, as usual, opened their doors and their hearts, and gave me press clippings and articles. It was good to talk over my ideas for this book. I like community input; it keeps me on track.

Through my journal, I'm attempting to show you, my reader, the process I'm going through as I write about child poverty.

After doing all this preliminary research, I did my first interview with a child today. It was really spontaneous. I was spending time at the Carnegie Community Centre, having a coffee, and I saw Paul. I have known Paul for many many years. He's sixteen and he and his family have always lived below the poverty line.

❖

I have had two major surgeries in the last seven months. Part of my therapy is to go three times a week to the local pool and do a water exercise class. Yesterday I was talking to a woman in my class about my book. S said, "I live below the poverty line, that's me . . . My daughter likes to draw. She's four years old. I'll ask her to do a sketch for you." S told me that when she was a child she was very poor and had to work six days a week delivering newspapers. She said, "You know, I never got to keep the money. My parents used it. The money was kept in a big jar. It was hard work."

Yesterday I interviewed three children. They were sisters, three, five, and six years old. We were at an anti-poverty group's annual meeting and there was a lot of food around. The children kept saying, "Can we eat now? Can we eat? I want to eat now." So the interviews were kind of short, very different from the one I did with Paul. I know that each child will take his or her interview in a different direction. I won't be able to ask each the same questions.

I was feeling so miserable, totally wiped out. There is something so special, so vulnerable about children; it's impossible not to be extremely concerned about the ones I talk to, and I get involved emotionally from the innermost parts of my body and mind. I have just finished interviewing Patty, a sweet, bright eleven-year-old who lives partly on the street, partly at home, and partly in a group home. She said children are not toys like video games and tapes. You can't just pick them up and play with them, then leave them. I interviewed her at a community centre. While I was talking to her, a staff person came up and said, "You are a truant. You are not supposed to be here. You are supposed to be in school. You can only come in this building after three-thirty." She replied, "I'm here with my mother. She's downstairs." He: "I don't care. You should be in school." Patty said she wished there was a place that was safe to go, off the street, where she wouldn't get busted.

The interview bothered me. What was I supposed to do? Use her for my book and then forget her? I can't do that. But I also can't break my promise of anonymity. She told me she would go to school tomorrow. I said perhaps I could meet her after school at the community centre. She said she would bring me some drawings she had done.

I did meet Patty the next day. I was so happy that she had gone back to school. The plan is for her to return to her family soon.

She brought me some of her sketches and writings. She is really talented. I told her she could be a really good writer if she wanted. She replied, "I like writing poetry." I gave her a hug and my phone number, and told her to keep in touch. She only stayed a few minutes. How she reminded me of me, when I was a runaway.

❖

When I was researching *Under the Viaduct,* I interviewed staff from the City of Vancouver's Social Planning Department and talked to the city's child advocate. I was told that there were plans to create a safe place for street kids to go, a place where they wouldn't be busted but would have a few days to think about "which way they were going." There's a new child advocate at City Hall now. I called and asked what had happened with the safe house. She said, "It didn't happen. They never got the funding." I have to check this out. Two years ago everyone was supporting this idea, all the agencies and government departments were on-side, and the funding seemed to be in place. Why did it fall through?

There's a real need for a place for young people to go. I talked with a staff person at the community centre where I had interviewed Patty, and asked about the policy of not allowing children in during school hours. He replied, "It's a real problem. We can't encourage children to hang out here during school hours, but when we make them leave, they go out onto the street and are vulnerable to the drug and sex trade out there. There's nowhere for us to send them to." I asked, "Couldn't we meet with Social Planning and see what happened to the safe house project?" He replied, "If you can get them here, sure, I'd come."

It seems that, as I write, it's impossible not to look at solutions. It's impossible not to want to do something about it. I'm aware that there are many people working to eliminate child poverty. People have presented briefs, studies, ideas . . . great, but where the hell is the safe house??

Jeff Brooks of the city's Social Planning Department called me about it. He said it had taken four years to get a detox residential program for youth, and that it was well used (but see John Turvey's interview on page 152). He was really disappointed that in spite of all the community and social services, and street children's planning for a safe house, the provincial government had turned down the funding request. He didn't know why. He said it is really needed. There's one in Victoria, and others in Alberta and Ontario, but they are too big. He felt that the solution isn't to "warehouse children" in a big institution. He says there are many people out there who are pushing for this safe house to happen.

I also spoke to Libby Davies, one of Vancouver's city counsellors, about the safe house. Even though it was a provincial decision, she still took the time to explain to me what was happening. Because the provincial government had turned funding requests down, there was no point in City Hall looking for a house that there was no funding for – it was to be a joint project. She agreed with me that there should be such a house, and she was glad that I did care enough to check it out. The request is being resubmitted. Perhaps it will still happen. I'll keep checking.

June

I'm going through the will-it-work-or-won't-it-work syndrome, scared that perhaps I won't be able to get enough interviews or that I won't be able to pull them all together in a book form that's acceptable.

I was talking with my daughter who is a daycare teacher. She said, "Mom, there are many parts to child poverty. What about recreation? Recreation equips children with good skills, yet recreation costs money." (I know that it costs a bundle for the swimming lessons, skating lessons, gymnastics, music, baseball, snow sports, and everything else that my grandchildren do.) "It's only when children who are poor are placed in foster care that they may get some of this stuff. When food and rent and clothes are top priority, there's little left for lessons." My daughter pointed out that if there are Boys' and Girls' Clubs in the area, it helps, but is it enough?

So there's another thing to think about – does a child who is poor have the right to good recreation?

I have two sources of children's sketches promised to me. One worker from a school in a low-income area does art therapy. She has promised me essays and sketches for September. Crabtree Corners' daycare has promised some too. Sandy Cameron, a retired teacher (he wrote the poverty curriculum for schools), is a really good friend who I always talk to about my books. I asked him about education and child poverty. He promised to get something together for me. So this is the process I'm going through as I write this book.

I have been hanging out, sometimes at Carnegie Centre in the downtown eastside, at La Quena on Commercial Drive where many of Vancouver's Latin American refugees go, at Crumbles, a coffee shop near my home in the West End, and at McDonald's on the Granville Mall. These are the places I meet and talk with children and youth, especially street kids. Street children. I have been trying to use the word children to give these children more dignity and respect.

It's the same as my other books; I want to get the real thing, spontaneous and unedited and straight from the heart. Giving these children a voice of their own is where it's at for me.

Child of the street
Excited by the lights
Turned on by the freedom
from dos and don'ts
Free at last
To sleep in the cold

To be hassled by creeps
To come off of a stone
To feel hunger and pain
When the lights go out
and the crowd's all gone
Waiting the dawn
On a bug-infested bed
Sleeping in doorways
No change of clothes
One second a tough guy
The next minute a child
Can you really blame me
For wanting you safe
From the cold and the creeps
and the dangers you face?
How can I not care?
Child of the street
I care
I do

❖

Patty introduced me to a friend, Tammy, a seventeen-year-old who had a one-year-old child in foster care and was visibly pregnant with another child. She had been on the street for many years. After the interview, which Patty sat in on, I said, "Let me know when the baby comes." Tammy replied, "Sure, that would be great," as she got in the elevator.

While Tammy was talking to me, she kept looking at Patty. Patty kept her eyes down, looking at her hands. I felt Tammy was talking to Patty as much as to me, warning her, telling her, "Don't do what I did."

❖

I haven't written much these last few days. It has been very difficult to sleep, to relax, to turn off.

My son said to me today, "Mom, are you sure you are going to be able to finish this book? Because I don't think so. You seem to be taking things really hard. It's as if you want to help every child you hear about. And you won't be able to do that. I think it's getting to you."

Patty said children are not toys. I wonder, is that how she sees me – interviewing her, then forgetting her? I think of that as the title of my book: "A Child is Not a Toy," a quote from Patty.

How am I going to make this book something that readers will read and then want to do something about, to make changes? There is so much research proving that poverty is the common denominator in child neglect and abuse. Isn't society abusing children by abandoning them, throwing them away?

I have been giving a lot of thought to, and doing a lot of reading about, First Nations children and poverty. The facts of this poverty are horrendous. I do not want to be another white person writing about First Nations issues, so I talked with some local native activists and asked their advice. They agreed that an in-depth study of native poverty must be written by the native people themselves, so for information on child poverty – or poverty in general – affecting the First Nations, please look for research done by them, for them. But if someone wanted to tell me their story, that was their choice. Some of the people whose interviews are in this book are native people, but I didn't identify them as native unless they spoke about it themselves.

My friend Joan is a social worker. She worked in family protection, dealing with child neglect, abuse, etc. How she hated her job. She had a huge caseload. She seldom had time to meet with the children that were in care, that were her responsibility. She often had to make judgment calls on families that she hardly had enough time to evaluate. Many of her children were faced with a constant turnover of staff due to overwork and burnout. So she quit and went to Calgary.

This week she phoned me. She is now with a volunteer association that works with child prostitutes, addicts, street kids. She is a house mother, earns a token wage, and feels that the group she is working with has a real contact with street youth.

When I told her about my book, she invited me to visit Calgary and stay at one of the houses and interview some of the children and youths staying at the house. "That would be a hell of a long bus ride," I thought, and I started to argue with myself about the pros and cons of going, and what about my back (which is an ongoing saga)? Where would I find the fare? etc.etc. This is one time that I feel it would be great to have some money that covered expenses. Anyway, we will see what happens.

❖

When I'm on the bus at night, I pass a blue bus on Granville Street. It is used by a group that comes out to feed the hungry. I look at the line-up. It is so long, and there are so many young people in the line. Every day there are more and more youngsters panhandling on the corners.

How many decades of hungry children have stared with their noses pressed to the bakery window? How many have walked down food aisles in supermarkets with a hungry belly but no money to buy? How many hungry children have looked into restaurants with eyes that showed their deep frustration? How long will it be before something triggers a riot, before the people start smashing windows, taking all the goodies that have been denied them for so long?

July

In *Under the Viaduct* a parent with two children talked about how hard it was to find housing on a welfare budget. Their rented house had been sold. The children were in foster care and then part-time care, with the family in a shelter. This was very difficult for the children. It was a problem for a very long time.

I heard some good news from this family. They are now living in a townhouse. It is social housing and it's out of town. I talked to Annie, the four-year-old, on the phone.

I am getting more confident that the book is going to happen. I have gathered quite a few interviews in the last month, and have started to collect sketches from children. Most, at the moment, seem to revolve around food and the lack of it and the worrying about it.

I asked one teenager for an interview. She got really pissed off and said, "Why? Nobody cares. The poor don't care about the rich and the rich don't care about the poor. Forget it," she said angrily.

I saw Patty's family yesterday. I asked how Patty was. Apparently she's home now.

❖

Yesterday I went to meet Alex. She has the most bubbly personality and is just 5. We met at English Bay and the thing she wanted to do the most was "the chocolate ice cream," so we went to have some ice cream.

She had brought me two sketches that she had done. She and her family live on Vancouver Island. Her family lives way below the poverty line. Alex told me that "poor" meant not having money to live in a house and not having money for food. She told me she wasn't poor because she lived in a house and she had food. Alex said to me, "I like shopping. I like shopping for pretty clothes at thrift stores."

I was at my WetFit class this week, soaking in the whirlpool with two other people after our exercises. We discussed poverty and education, food and special activities like music that poor children can't afford to do. One parent said, "That's why I go to food banks, because I use some of my food money to send my children to music and dance classes. I want them to grow up with expectations in life." We agreed that I could go over and visit them the following Thursday. That's how the best interviews happen, just by hanging out, talking to people, telling them what I'm trying to do. I really don't know where the book will take me. It's like a stream full of twists and bends. My job is to follow it faithfully as it flows.

I went to visit my family in the Okanagan for a few days. I found myself in a children's dress-up parade that went up and down the main street. Children in costumes marched happily down the street with their parents. There were balloons and clowns, happy, happy faces. I was right there in the middle, pushing my two-year-old grandson. I had pencilled a moustache and beard on his face, and gave him a toy guitar and a large hat. There we were marching in a children's parade. Then it hit me. This was the first parade I had ever been in "just for the fun of it." I've marched with women's groups and labour unions, for protests and for every kind of rights, but this warm day in July was the very first time I had been in a march for fun!

I tried hard not to think too much about which of the smiling children knew hunger and poverty. Some did, that's for sure. I feel comfortable with the fact that I enjoyed the happy smiling faces of those children. If society really wanted to change its attitude and love all children, then there would be numerous happy parades of laughing children who are not hungry, who live in decent housing, who feel secure.

❖

I interviewed children from three young families today, families that struggled with food banks, poverty, and the frustration that it brings. For families on welfare, this month is a five-week month. The cheque that is already 50 percent below the poverty line must stretch another week. The children don't always know they are poor, and if they do, they don't know why. They do, however, pick up the fear, the worry, as they see the stressed-out adults who are trying to cope with survival. One small girl was worried that there was no money for popsicles, mommy had no money for popsicles. She also said that's why you steal popsicles, when there's no money to buy them.

Two of these families insisted on sharing their supper with me. Barbara told me about her childhood poverty. She said she seldom had clean underwear as a child, and was treated really badly in school. This made me remember that I too had very little underwear. In fact, I remember having sugar bags that were sewn together as underwear. They were rough, and the legs were not even sewn. I was teased unmercifully at school. I shared this with Barbara. If people are going to talk about their pain, then I must always be honest and expose mine.

When I came home, I had to transfer from one bus to another, it was pouring rain, it was late, my head was full of painful memories, and I was also remembering the pain of the interviews. I was really down, so I bought this sticky icky chocolate thing that had fudge in it. It was gross, and didn't do anything to stop the pain.

What seems to help is the noise of my fingers banging this typewriter as I let it out instead of burying it. This is my third book, and each time I let out a little it helps me find myself.

August

I called Social Planning to see what's happening with the safe house for runaway children. Jeff Brooks had some good news, but he cautioned me: Nothing is reality until you have the money in your hand for it, he said. Groups are meeting and talking about the hows and whys and whose is it and where would it be if we had it? It is definitely being negotiated.

It seems to me that many people care, many groups are working on the problem of street kids, but the solutions are slow in materialising. We are still making the same mistakes. Society must really take a good look at how poverty is affecting our children's lives. This situation has been eroding our communities.

I was talking with a nine-year-old boy. He is really bright. He said people are poor because we send our stuff down to the United States and they sell it back to us for more money. We should keep our own stuff, he said.

A pattern seems to be forming, one that I relate to on a personal level. Children whose families are poor go to school, they feel different, feel ashamed, embarrassed, scared that friends will know that they are poor. They feel they don't belong, that teachers don't like them because they are poor. They feel jealous of other children who have what they would like to have. They feel alone and isolated. I am an adult. I have grown children, and grandchildren. I have friends. Yet I seldom lose that feeling of not belonging, not being part of . . . whatever it is at that moment I would like to be part of.

My five-year-old grandson Bobby said, "Grandma, it's my birthday and I'm gonna give my money to the poor. I'm rich, I've got all these pennies. I want to give them to the poor." He and my other grandchildren have been around me and my work. I asked him, "How do you think a poor family feels when they have no money to buy food?" He said, "Hungry. They must feel hungry.

They can have my pennies, Grandma. I'm rich, I have all these pennies . . . "

❖

In the *Province* on August 18, 1992, the headline says "Family forced to split after mother dies – Child care plight shared by many Canadian families." A thirty-year-old woman died from cancer with the pain of knowing her three sons, all under the age of six, were living with friends in three different locations. Her husband worked shifts, so was unable to look after the children.

The largest ever study of childcare, released last week, found that only 55 percent of working parents had a nine-to-five, Monday-to-Friday job. I ask myself, if daycares operate from nine to five, Monday through Friday, yet only 55 percent of families have those hours, where do children go if their parents are working shifts?

❖

Many of the children that I talk with say that their teachers don't like poor children, that they are picked on. I asked one teacher, Marlene Baker, who is a friend of mine, about this. She said it could be possible but she hadn't been aware of it. One interesting thing she did say was that she always wears touchable clothes to school, clothes that are easily washed. Some teachers may wear more expensive clothes, and they don't want dirty, sticky little hands touching them, so that could possibly make a child feel the teacher didn't like them.

I met a real neat woman called Lorna Bennett. She's a child psychologist in the school system. She agreed with what poor children had told me. She felt that some teachers were treating poor children differently, perhaps judgmentally, and perhaps some were not even aware that they were doing it. We discussed my firm belief that a poverty curriculum should be taught in school, giving children a healthy, non-judgmental classroom.

The principal of one school said to me, "Remember Sheila, there are middle-class and rich children too that are deprived of love and attention."

❖

We agreed to meet in a Greek restaurant on Broadway near Kingsgate Mall. I was apprehensive; she was the daughter of a friend from Montreal, a wonderful woman that I have known for years. I have known her daughter for a long time too, but this was the first I'd heard of the abuse that she had experienced because the family was poor when she was a child. I wondered how my friend would react, how she would feel – although I know she would be proud of the poem her daughter had written in praise of her. She had written her story, the pain of when she was a poor child in school, of the sexual abuse and how she had survived it. We read it together over the Greek salad we shared. Her writing was scratched out, hand-written. I told her that was how I wrote, straight from the heart. I looked at the blue-checkered curtains, so cheerful, as we read together of the pain she went through when she was only seven. The salad lost its taste. The curtains looked dull. The waitress asked, "Can I get you something else?" We both said, "No thank you." We talked at length until the waitress felt obliged to come and interrupt us with, "May I bring you your bill?" We hugged and parted company, both with tears in our eyes. My legs felt wobbly and I shivered as I went to catch the bus on Main Street. She waved and walked swiftly away, head down. My heart went out to her and her mother. Truths sometimes hurt, but burying them is worse.

Later that day I saw Patty, dressed in a baseball hat, a pair of old runners, jeans. She looked like an average eleven-year-old. It's always good to see her.

❖

I received a call from B.C. Bookworld telling me my last book, *Under the Viaduct*, had won an award from VanCity Credit Union and the Ministry of Women's Equality. This gave a real lift to my self esteem. My fingers attack the typewriter with enthusiasm. It feels good to have the stories in my book validated; that somehow validates the messages that my books deliver to the reader, to you.

Yet fear comes. Fear of not deserving success. Memory flips back to a scene in school. The only thing I did really well at age nine was read. I read everything I could get my hands on. The library was my oasis. We had an English test at school. We had to write in all the punctuation on a piece of writing. Of course, being a reader, I scored perfectly – the only time I ever did. The teacher went around the room to see who had the highest score.

When she found out it was me, she said, "It couldn't possibly be you. You are lying! Let me see your paper. You couldn't possibly have scored that high." She was angry, her face full of fury. She never did admit that I had done well. The memory fills me with sadness for the little girl with a dirty neck and dirty fingernails. I ask myself, "Is this the reason I am feeling fear at getting this award?"

❖

There is a bonding that seems to happen when two people, be they women, men, or children, share past pains and survivals of the roller coaster of life. I'm aware that adults and children come and go with their stories in my last two books; some of the same adults or their children are in this book – brief moments in their lives, sometimes longer, are shared with me and my readers. As usual, there is no ending, no literary pattern, no attempt to entertain. Real life is seldom sewn up in neat little packets as in fiction. You may often wonder what happened to this person? What was the result, what was the ending? Some I may know, but most I don't.

❖

Youth crime is increasing rapidly, the news announcer said.

One woman told me her son said, "Mom, I got myself out of poverty. I'm dealing drugs."

She said she hoped he was joking.

Patty's family told me that Patty had been waiting for over a year to get into sexual abuse therapy, but now she has finally started. For the time being, she's staying in a group home. She is a really bright child with so much potential, but I have never seen her smile.

September

It's back-to-school time. I shopped with my daughter for my ten-year-old grandson's long list of school supplies. It's expensive. "No Mom, it's got to be leather runners. Just nobody wears runners that are not leather." I thought about the working poor parents who have the same lists and the same pressure, about the kids who wouldn't get the stuff on the list. I thought about the children on assistance. I wonder, will the children who can't buy what's on the list, who don't have the right clothes, find someone in the school system who will help them and their classmates know that education doesn't depend on clothes? If a child hasn't got all the supplies, will the school be able to provide them? Will society, the system, stop labelling a child as a Welfare Child from a Welfare Home? These labels are inappropriate. A child is a child and a home is a home. The media does this all the time, headlines and news stories will scream WELFARE MOM, WELFARE FAMILY, WELFARE KID. Why don't we say WELFARE MULRONEY? His money comes from the same kitty, from the taxpayer, as does the money for all the other government services and employees. Sorry if I seem to be preaching, but it really pisses me off.

❖

The Sunday *Province* has a story about a woman in a wheelchair, Vicky Nicholson, a panhandler, who is helping homeless street kids. She says, "I hurt for these kids. They're so hungry they're turning to stealing." She said people are scared to come to Granville because at least fifty kids are panhandling. Some are as young as twelve. She said the number of kids has tripled in the last four years.

The article says some street kids have turned to drugs and alcohol, some have been sexually assaulted. Because they had no money for bus fare, they hitchhike and that's when assaults happen.

Nicholson said, "I feel sad for a lot of these kids. They're stealing and selling drugs because they can't feed their bellies."

There is a fairly new group, Quest, that feeds the homeless. They seem to be different from other soup kitchens. They are volunteers and just collect money for food supplies. They give food with dignity, no strings attached, a real meal with salads, meat or fish, and dessert. One homeless person said, "Some of the other places put on a big spread at Christmas, call in the media, collect donations, then feed you swill the rest of the time." I've been around Quest when they have been cooking, and the food sure looks and smells good.

❖

I had a discussion with a social worker who works in the school system in Winnipeg. She agreed that poor children were tested and evaluated by a system that wasn't really accurate. What a child has been exposed to is going to affect any testing, and middle-class or rich children who have had lessons and other enriched experiences would do well in kindergarten testing. She said that children who were never encouraged to read books, or who never had the role model of people reading books, were slower to learn to read.

The woman got a little nervous about doing an interview. She said, "You know, this is very political, very political. I have to be careful. I can't tread on anyone's toes. I have to work you know. I have a family."

Poverty and children and the education system are political, and people must accept that changes must come . . . and toes will be trodden on (maybe even amputated)!

She called me back the next day and said she had got permission from her boss to write something for me. I told her I wasn't interested in textbook theories. I was looking for people who were prepared to speak out for change. She asked how she could work effectively with the teachers if she alienated them. I told her, "That's why we are in such a mess as a society; people protect their jobs, scared to speak out about abuse." She said she would mail me something. If it's relevant it will be in the book. If you don't see it, then it wasn't boat-rocking material.

❖

Many parents, after a lot of thought, decide not to let their children be interviewed. Many children themselves say no way. I have accepted this, as I knew this was the way it would be. I wonder, if someone had asked me to let my children be interviewed about poverty when they were small, what would I have said? I would have had serious questions about it. I'm grateful, however, to those who allow their children to be in this book.

The sketches have been a wonderful way for young children to express themselves. Children who are too young to write still see and hear, and they are extremely aware. Through the sketches I have been able to see life through their eyes.

I wonder, with anticipation, what the next months will bring, which direction this book will take? As long as I let go and flow with it, opportunities open up. Hanging out, meeting people, I do a lot of phoning, getting really intimate with what I'm doing, going really deep into the truth, being aware, of course, of my limitations, and of boundaries that I or others set up.

I understand there are about 300 children living on the streets in Vancouver. I want to talk to some nurses in the youth clinics about the health of these children. I already know that children in poverty have more diseases, die more frequently, and drop out of school more often, and they have health problems that are related directly to poverty.

I was talking to a doctor who works with the clinics, and asked him about the safe house. This doctor felt there was a need for a place where children, even if they were from a group home or a foster home, could have time out to think. The problem, the doctor explained, is there are other priorities to do with children. One of the few places to get money for a safe house is through the Ministry of Social Services. But that means that the safe house would only be available for children aged sixteen and older, who are eligible for social assistance, and who do not have to be apprehended and returned home when they are found on the street. I guess all the bureaucrats understand this, and it must seem logical to them, but to me it doesn't make sense. If a fifteen-year-old, or a ten or five-year-old needs this service, why shouldn't it be available to them?

I was in Chinatown today with my friend Lee, shopping for fish and medicinal herbs. While I was there, I met Patty. She hugged me. She seemed to have grown taller. She was with a younger friend. Patty asked me excitedly, "Do you have your tapedeck with you?" I excused myself from Lee and took off with the girls to a nearby library to do an interview. Patty said she was doing fine, that she was going back to school but staying in a group home. I asked her how the sexual abuse therapy was going. She said, "I don't really talk about it. I call it play therapy. You should talk to my friend here – she sure has been sexually abused."

Turning to her friend she said, "You want to be in her book? She won't say who you are, you know. You can use another name." I introduced myself to Patty's friend and said, "You know, I was abused when I was a child, too, and I was in foster homes. I understand."

❖

I talked with John Turvey at Downtown Eastside Youth Activities Society. He is outspoken, pulls no punches, and often disagrees with solutions proposed by other social workers or child activists. I don't believe that everyone I interview has to agree on solutions. They all agree on the problem, and agree that something has to be done, even if they have different ideas for the solution.

I'm a terrible typist and a worse speller, so it took quite a long time to transcribe Turvey's interview, listening to the tape over and over, making sure I captured his voice accurately, and that I heard him correctly.

I rage and fret all day, feeling powerless until my fingers grab at the typewriter and scream out, "Please please readers of this book, take some action, do something." Why do these children continue to be victimized by us? Why should these children have to wait so long for sexual abuse counselling? Why? Why? Why? If they had money there are all kinds of therapists available at a hundred bucks an hour. Should these children turn tricks maybe, so that they can afford a shrink? $100 for a trick and $100 for a therapist.

My fingers on the typewriter . . . my brain, for the moment, can hardly see a light at the end of the tunnel, yet I know people are reading my books. I know that they care and they want change too. As I said, it's political. It's midnight and I want to sleep, yet I think and think about those children.

❖

On the positive side, my friend Marlene Baker introduced me to some of her friends. One man told me he came from a very poor family in Saskatchewan. There were eight children. They lived on a farm. They didn't know they were poor until they were bussed in to school. People from the community helped them all adjust. Their parents read with them every night. He said proudly, "We all made it. We all have professions, and I am a teacher."

❖

I met a woman called Naomi at La Quena, and had a brief conversation with her. "I work in a residential home for children, for children in care," she said. "Since children have been encouraged to speak up about sexual abuse there has been so many disclosures that there just isn't staff enough or services out there to handle it. Children have to wait and wait.

"We had one child who was acting out, angry, difficult. She had been abused. It took so long to get help and she was a ward of the state. Something has to be done soon. There is just not enough resources. Children were encouraged to disclose abuse, but the services to help them are just not enough. I think no one estimated how much abuse of children there is. It's just pouring out."

I met a woman who had been living in shelters with her daughters. I have known her a long time. She said, "Sheila, I have a wonderful co-op home now. It's so nice! Why couldn't I have had it when my children were younger. It's almost too late for two of them." It makes me depressed to think about it.

Being homeless and in shelters has contributed to some children becoming runaways and living on the street. What changes can we make to prevent this? How do we keep a child's self esteem intact while he or she is in a shelter?

Penny Parry, the child advocate for Vancouver, came to see me at my apartment. She had promised me some information on the elusive safe house, and I couldn't close the book without updating the information. It seems the safe house will happen, but it will be for young people, sixteen years old and up. She felt that at least it was a start. I know how I feel about it, but I'll leave you to form your own conclusion.

Penny gave me the name of a police officer to talk to about some of the things that have come up in the book, the questions about why it takes so long for sexually abused children to get help, and why it often takes a long time for alleged abusers to be prosecuted. I was told that I would be able to interview someone with knowledge of that department.

Penny is working on "equity of input and outcome" for children. This is the same thing that the Winnipeg social worker told me about: some children start school with skills that they have developed from their environment – from being around books, going to libraries, travelling, good nutrition, a safe environment, classes in various things like music, dance, gymnastics, receiving lots of positive attention, etc. Some children have few of these experiences and when they come to school, it is often not in an affluent area. Even the schools don't have equity of input. Somehow we have to balance things so that no children are left behind.

The question I ask myself is, how is it going to be done with dignity so that a child who is poor doesn't feel labelled? I understand the need, but I'm also aware of labels that fulfill themselves. How do we get equity of outcome?

I think they had the same idea when I was a child in east London, England. We were taken to classical concerts and shown all the different instruments. I would never have heard classical music otherwise. We also went to different factories to see how happy factory workers were. Yeah, sure. Perhaps they were teaching us to be happy factory workers who like classical music.

The most positive memories for me are when an adult, teacher or otherwise, took the time to listen to me, to treat me with kindness and caring, to make positive statements about me, showing me they liked me by their tone of voice or their eyes and their body language.

October

My last book won a prize, so I now have some extra tools for my work, one of which is a camera. It's fun trying to take pictures that I think are relevant to the stories – if you see some really amateur snaps in this book, please be patient and remember it's the subject matter that I want to show, not the art form.

I ran into Paul, the young man I interviewed in May, so I asked him what had been happening for him since we last talked. It's difficult to see this talented, bright young person stuck in the poverty cycle and out of school at sixteen. He wants to be in the music trade, but jobs don't pay enough for him to take the courses he wants. I have seen him perform and sing since he was a wee one, and he's good.

The governments are talking cutbacks again. For the last twenty years I have been a community activist, and the community has always pleaded for budget money to be spent on preventative work. I wonder how many people have given up, are in jail, are the second and third generation of a family living on assistance? How many people will give up trying to work because minimum wage is not enough to rent an apartment and buy food and the necessities of life. Families need the right tools to raise children, the opportunity for good, affordable daycare, for decent jobs, rent controls, and an easier way to buy a house. I say to myself, "Slow down, Sheila, you sound like you are ranting." Maybe I am.

❖

I've always been an anti-poverty activist and I've used the same rules to write my books as I used when I worked as a community organizer in Montreal: talk to the grassroots people, find out what they say the need or the problem is, document it, research it, find other people who have the same or similar concerns, help them have a voice, help them prove where the needs are and what solutions they think are needed. In the end, that makes a healthier community of people – they can see that it's a social problem, not a personal one. Some workers are scared to speak up; how I admire the courage and ethics of the ones that do.

I'm at the stage of putting my interviews and sketches and pictures in some kind of sequence to make up the manuscript. It's quite exciting, but sad, too. The stories are often sad, but the fact that these children are going to have a voice excites me. You know there is a lot of crap going on around kids. If we try to hide it the smell will get worse and diseases will come, so it's healthier, I think, to look at the crap and try and deal with it.

❖

I saw Paul again. He is such a fine person. I first wrote about Paul in *No Way to Live* in 1988. He was eleven then, and living way below the poverty line with his family. I gave him a different name in this book to protect his privacy. That way he can choose who he wants to tell that he is in the book.

Patty's family was also in *Under the Viaduct*. I didn't meet Patty, but her family talked with me about their experiences in shelters and transitions houses.

Poverty hasn't changed much since those books were written. It's just much more difficult to stretch a dollar with the GST and all the rent increases, and when a person buys something like an appliance, hell, they hardly last a minute. They seem to be programmed to malfunction so that a person has to replace them.

I'm aware that the power of the world has become money. This book has been about what's happening around me, and what's happening around me is affected and controlled eventually by world economic policies. A depressing thought.

❖

I'm amazed as I look back on my journal at the things I have learned. It was like setting out on a journey. I had no idea where the book would take me. I just knew I wanted to give poor children a voice. I stayed flexible, opened doors and looked in, opened cans of worms and asked "why?" The truth is, it's worse than I thought it was.

I never knew there were so many poor children who had to wait so long to get the help they needed. Often help came when it was too late.

I have also learned that there are many people out there who care and want changes. And I know that when I put it all down in a book, the speakers get a chance to be heard, to speak out. I guess there is a real positive thought, and that is that libraries will have these books for years, so the truth will be preserved in the written word.

❖

I talked to the police about the possibility of an interview. I explained to them the problems children that are poor are faced with in the courts system. They are going to call me back.

I was doing some volunteer work in the West End of Vancouver. Kate, a bright, intelligent, outgoing young girl was working with me. We laughed and talked and became friends. It turned out that she was one of the Youth Works trainees who was learning how to "get off the street and start over" (as their slogan says). She had been a runaway and had been part of the Granville Street scene. I asked her if I could interview her for my book. She replied, "Sure, I'd love to." She is an example of what can happen when people care. She later introduced me to Maggie Duckett, the Youth Works coordinator. It was such a confirmation for me to find myself working with the very person I was looking to interview, someone with a message to give.

❖

I'm still trying to get an interview with the Vancouver Police sexual abuse team. A policeman in community relations told me there were some internal reviews going on that may not be finished in the next couple of weeks, and because of this they were not in a position to discuss the number of workers or how their system worked. He sounded like he would really try to get me the interview. It sounds like something serious is happening within the department.

One of my last interviews was with Michael, an executive director of an agency that is contracted to work with kids. He had some ideas that I didn't agree with, and I wondered if they should be in this book. But some of his ideas make some sense. Should I leave out those I don't agree with? I decided that my readers can accept or disagree with anyone in this book, so his ideas are there, even if I don't agree with them.

In B.C. I am aware that the present NDP government inherited a huge deficit from the previous Social Credit government, not to mention that the Progressive Conservative federal government has done little to erase child poverty except cut funds for social programs and support. It grows steadily worse as the gap between rich and poor widens, and more and more of the so-called middle class finds itself out of work or taxed into the category of the working poor.

The B.C. government has made some changes in the welfare system that help families a little, but it's just not enough. Single parents may now get $50 for transportation expense to childcare when they start a job, job-start costs up to $200 for miscellaneous expenses when starting a full time job, work clothes expenses, and job training.

One improvement is that the Employment Opportunity Program has been changed. Under the old program, the employers paid $3.50 an hour and the ministry paid $3.50, so the most a worker could get was $7 an hour. You can't pay rent and support a family on that. Under the new program, the employer has to pay minimum wage of $5.50, and the government will top it up by $3.50 an hour. Now a worker can get $9 an hour, but that's still not enough to raise a family.

There's a new program aimed at young people, age fifteen to twenty-four, in care – Youth Employment Skills. It's another wage supplement program, and as with EOP, the jobs created are not permanent, so it's a bandaid, but at least it gives children and youth a chance to work, to learn some job skills, to make some money and feel some self-confidence.

Is there a light at the end of the tunnel? I'm not really sure.

I have to give the present B.C. government one thing: they are approachable, visible, and do meet with the communities, and they seem to really care about fundamental issues such as pollution and the environment, peace, women's rights, poverty . . . but even so, we must be ever on guard, never letting go of our issues. For me, it's child poverty. Canada is just not doing enough. We as a community are not doing enough. Are you doing enough? Am I?

❖

I am trying to get a real understanding of child labour. What I see and what the law says seem to be different. Some of the youth that I have already interviewed feel frustrated with the low-paying jobs and they question why they should be paid less than adults for the same work. Paul wants a job that would provide medical and dental benefits. Many young people are locked into part-time jobs that have no benefits and no future. Employers get away without paying benefits when an employee is a part-time worker, and they pay a lower wage if the employee is under fifteen years old. Other countries in Europe, I am told, protect their youth and encourage education. I talked to Dennis Gornell, from the Ministry of Labour, Employment Standards Branch. According to the 1969 updated legislation, for employment purposes, a child is someone under fifteen years of age. They are no longer a child at fifteen. To hire a child under the age of fifteen, the employer must apply for a special permit. Youth are paid only $5 an hour, but minimum wage for adults is $5.50. Some fast-food outlets make a point of hiring thirteen to fifteen year olds.

❖

I just talked to a social worker from the Ministry of Social Services (MSS). She was really guarded in her responses, saying she couldn't be quoted in my book, but that she would tell me some of the general stuff about street kids, sexually transmitted diseases, malnutrition. I was aware of her doing the social worker bit on me – the voice, the authority. We clashed. I asked her if she felt that these children got everything they needed. She said they didn't, and she was concerned about it, but she couldn't be quoted.

I told her I thought that since the NDP got in, the muzzles were off. I said goodbye, I'll get back to you, but I was feeling sad because this person had a chance to really speak up and out. I didn't understand why she said I could interview her but not quote her. I felt really frustrated when I hung up the phone. But she is answerable to her supervisors.

Later, I had a chance to ask Mike Harcourt, the NDP premier, about this when he was in Vancouver for a Carnegie Community Centre anniversary. He said that it's hard for some workers to change their mindset, even with a new government in power, but he told me to "keep on asking questions." But I wonder, should I have to be the one to fight and argue? Can't the government tell its workers to be more open, that social workers are free to fight for their clients' rights? Unless of course they're not free.

January

It's January, and a few final pieces of information trickle in. I got a few answers from the Vancouver Police. There are ten detectives on the sexual abuse squad, including two women, as well as a sergeant and staff-sergeant. They were asked to investigate 751 complaints in 1992, but could not give me information on how many cases were prosecuted or convicted, how many were dropped, nor were there statistics about the age and sex of the complainants.

I've been reading the two huge reports MSS commissioned on family and child services in B.C. – "Making Changes: A Place to Start" and "Liberating Our Children, Liberating Our Nations," which is specifically on First Nations issues. Two panels went out into B.C. communities and really listened to the children, youth, parents, social workers, and others who work with and are concerned about children. They called for more community-based and family-based solutions to problems, more involvement of children in decisions affecting their lives, more continuity of care, so that children aren't bounced around between foster homes and family, and so that native children aren't placed with, or adopted by non-native families. Now we have to wait and see if the government will listen to them.

I've been getting a lot of help from people in the Communications Division at MSS. I asked for a report on what the government did for children during its first year in power, requesting that it only be a two or three-page summary (I know how long-winded politicians can be!). A few days later, the short summary, with information from other ministries as well as MSS, was faxed to my publisher.

The provincial government is going to raise the minimum wage and income assistance rates again. They *did* put a moratorium on the adoption of aboriginal children. The Ministry of Women's Equality wants to increase safe, affordable childcare, particularly for infants and toddlers. The new "Post Majority Services Program" is in place to help former wards of the state finish their education, even after they pass the age of 19, when, in the past, they were no longer the responsibility of MSS.

> Until recently, young people in the care of the Ministry of Social Services were 'discharged' from the *Family and Child Service Act* at nineteen years of age. We heard over and over again that 'real parents' don't abandon their children when they turn nineteen, and neither should the Ministry if it has become the legal parent.

> Expecting these young people to magically turn into self-sufficient young adults is unrealistic.
>
> "Making Changes: A Place to Start"

It sounds like some solutions may finally be on track. I hope so. It can't happen too soon. A *Province* article from January 24 says that the number of teens on welfare is up by more than half since 1990 – from 1,684 people to 2,634.

❖

In October 1991 I was lying on a bed at St. Paul's Hospital. There were staples making train tracks all the way down my right leg. My grandson had suggested I have a train tattooed on the future scar. I had had a knee replacement and it was bloody sore. Rolf, the publisher of New Star Books, had dropped by to give me a hug, even though he was busy as usual. We sat and talked. I expressed a desire to write about children who were poor, and said that I'd like to give them a voice . . . but I didn't think I had a right to do it because so many people were presently working so hard with child poverty groups. I thought that perhaps they would want to do a book. Rolf said, "Sheila, that would be a great sequel to your other books, and you know there's room for more than one book." I lay on the bed thinking, I would really like to do it. I was also feeling a little strange because of the painkillers and the morphine machine that was attached to my arm. Now it is little more than a year later, and the children's book is nearly finished because I was given so much encouragement from friends, family, fellow anti-poverty workers, and New Star Books. I can't believe it has happened so fast.

I'm told that my work is "folk art." I like that. Grandma Moses was great, and she was a late bloomer, too.

When I give this manuscript to my editor, I will part company with you, the reader. Thank you for reading my journal. It's not meant to be a scholarly piece of work, just a story of the book as it progressed. I didn't know what way it would take me, what paths it would lead me to. I never expected the school to play so large a role in how children see themselves in their poverty. The sexual abuse is there, and so few resources to deal with it when a child is poor.

As Patty said, a child is not a toy. I say, a book is not a solution. It's what you do with the book. Hear the children that cry out for help in this book. Hear them, help them. Help society change its attitude. Talk to governments and to corporations about paying decent wages. Make sure that poverty is understood in the school system, that children are taught not to blame themselves if there is no money for runners and no food for breakfast. Social workers, teachers, parents are sometimes stuck in the let's-not-rock-the-boat syndrome, let's not tread on anyone's toes. Let's not forget those who teach the teachers how to be teachers. Changes are needed. So please don't let this book just sit as a decoration on your bookshelf. Pass it on.

Please don't forget the children in this book.

If you are an adult and were an abused child, my heart goes out to you. Remember, it wasn't your fault.

It's so very hard to say this is the end. The phone rings. I meet someone who I just can't leave out of the book, and I open the journal again. I really should stop. Except to tell you that I was asked to be a guest as a writer at a run that children from two private schools were doing to raise money for Operation Eyesight. There I sat in that auditorium with about 450 children, some dressed in their red uniforms, others in navy. Friendly, noisy, sweet-faced kids, who were not poor, who had good runners and adequate money in the family for nutrition. They picked their noses, scratched their heads, acted out, just like any other children that I've seen. They were all just children, because a child is just a child.

POVERTY TRENDS, CHILDREN UNDER 18

Year	*Number of Children Under 18 Living in Poverty*	*Poverty Rate*
1980	984,000	14.9
1981	998,000	15.2
1982	1,155,000	17.8
1983	1,221,999	19.0
1984	1,253,000	19.6
1985	1,165,000	18.3
1986	1,086,000	17.0
1987	1,057,000	16.6
1988	987,000	15.4
1989	934,000	14.5
1990	1,105,000	16.9

CHILDREN UNDER 18 LIVING IN POVERTY IN 1990

Province	*Percent of Population*	*Number of Children*
Newfoundland	19.6	32,000
Prince Edward Island	13.7	5,000
Nova Scotia	16.5	35,000
New Brunswick	17.1	31,000
Quebec	18.1	292,000
Ontario	14.7	346,000
Manitoba	22.0	58,000
Saskatchewan	20.4	55,000
Alberta	18.3	124,000
British Columbia	16.9	128,000
Canada	16.9	1,105,000

Source: Both charts are from the National Council of Welfare, *Poverty Profile, 1980-1990.*

Interviews With Children

Kyle

Kyle, age four. His family lives below the poverty line.

❖

I'm not poor. Just my mom doesn't get a lot of money, not from anything. She's not rich.

What would you like to buy if you had money?

A basketball and hoop, a big truck for my friend – he's not grown up yet. Some juicy pears.

What kind of food would you buy?

Celery, milk, some cereal, Cheerios, chocolate milk, some ice cream, and some of that pink stuff with the white stuff on it. When I'm grown up, I will buy ice cream all the time.

Where will you get the money?

I don't know how you get it.

Ashley

Ashley, age eight. Her family lives below the poverty line.

❖

What does being poor mean?

You can't buy food. You don't have a place to live. You can't buy a Nintendo. You can't have nice clothes . . . You can't go to the movies . . . You can't do what you want to do.

Stevy, age eight

What changes would you like to make if you had the power?
I don't know, but the bank should give people money.

Annie

Annie, age four. Her family lives below the poverty line, and has been homeless. I interviewed her by telephone.

❖

What do we use money for?
Bubble gum, chips, cooking, curtains, TVs, books, and shoes.
What does being poor mean?
Poor . . . when you're poor you cry and cry. Burglars take all your money. Strangers take all your money.
How did you like the shelter you were in?
Too many rooms, eight . . . nine . . . ten. Too much time-out in my room for doing my own thing. Too many dumb kids . . . because they pulls your hair, hits you . . . slap you.

How do you like your new house?

I like it . . . I've got my own bedroom. There's three bedrooms, and I've got two new friends.

What do you dream about?

Carrots and rabbits, the baby rabbit got run over and the mommy rabbit cried and cried, and the giant sleeps in the castle with his eyes open in case the strangers come . . .

Patrick

Patrick, age four. His family lives above the poverty line

❖

Patrick, do you know what poor means?

Nope.

What do we use money for?

To buy stuff.

They want to be happy so they are not poor. Poor is not happy.

Alex, age five

Where does money come from?
The bank.
What if the bank doesn't have any money?
Silly, use the MasterCard.

Jane

Jane, age seven. Her family lives way below the poverty line.

❖

What do you think money is used for?

Lots of stuff. Clothes. If I had no money I would get them from friends. If somebody's poor, they don't have lots of money. They don't usually have a house. They just live out on the street. They probably wouldn't eat.

If I were a queen, I'd give them whatever they need. If they needed a house, I'd give them a house, and if they needed clothes, I'd give them clothes and money. I'd help all the poor people if I was a queen.

When I grow up I want to be a doctor or a lawyer.

How are you going to do that?

By going to school.

Veronica

Veronica, age eleven. Her family lives way below the poverty line.

❖

Poor means not to have any money and no home. They might not feel all that well, especially when people bug them about it. They would probably feel very sad and stuff. If they had a home, they would probably go to their home and just sit there by themselves, probably. Poor kids sometimes they might just play by themselves because no one wants to play with them. They probably get pretty lonely.

Why do people become poor?

I guess it's just because they didn't finish school and stuff. They quit really early. Then they didn't get jobs. They just gave up I guess. I'm going into Grade 6. I hope to be a business woman. I'll keep in school and I'll get my degree.

Me and my sister used to have this book, sort of a catalogue, we would flip through and we'd have different coloured pens and say, "that's mine, that's mine, that's mine," pretend that we had lots of money and then we would go and buy them.

How do you think poor children feel when they are in school?

They probably feel pretty sad because lots of kids pick on them, I guess. They probably get beat up and stuff.

If I was the boss of everything, I would make it so that there was no such thing as money. If you don't have any money then you can't get anything and stuff. I would like it if people . . . they could just go into a store and say, can I please get whatever, and then they could get it. Right now there is such a thing as money and everybody has money, and you have to have money. If you don't have money, then you can't get food and stuff. I would make it so that there wasn't any money. Then you wouldn't have to starve or go without certain clothes and stuff. They would have cows and stuff and they would trade stuff. Like two loaves of bread for some milk and stuff like that.

If I told you there was enough money to join any class that you wanted to join, what would you want to take?

If I could join any club or anything like that, I would want to join . . . I used to want to play the piano, but now I want to learn how to . . . paint and stuff, and draw. Gymnastics, you know like how they twirl around on that board thing? And also swimming, I want to learn how to swim really good. You know how they dance on TV, like the music videos? I would like to learn how to do some of that.

If you were a queen, what would you do?

If I were a queen I would get my workers to build all sorts of houses for everybody. I would make it so that everybody can live in my kingdom. Anybody who wanted to live there could live there.

I'll tell you a sorta sad story. Once upon a time there was a little girl and she lived with her mother and her grandma. And she knew a girl who only lived where she lived in the summer, and she knew a boy who only lived there in the winter, and so she only had a few friends. She would play with the girl every summer, and they would go swimming and stuff, and then in the winter her and the boy would make snowmen and stuff. They would also have snowball fights. Then one day her grandma died. They didn't have very much money, so they didn't have a very good funeral. But they did have a funeral for her. They had a casket and it was closed because it was too sad. Everybody brang flowers and stuff. And the girl and the boy came too because they knew the grandma very well. And then one summer day the two little girls thought that they saw her grandma. And the grandma came down and reached out to the girl and gave her a big hug and then the grandma went back up to heaven and the little girl knew for sure that her grandmother loved her. The End.

Samantha

Samantha, age eleven. Her family lives above the poverty line.

❖

I think being poor means having not a lot of money and not exactly living in good standards, being on welfare, maybe not even getting allowance and not getting as much toys as children above the poor line do.

There's a lot of poor kids at my school but I don't exactly know how many. My school has a lunch program because it's one of the poorest schools. The lunch program is set up for children that are poor. You put money in an envelope. You don't have to put any if you don't have any. You put as much as you can. Then you send it back to the school and you get lunches every day of the week for a month. The lunches are to have the kids not going with an empty stomach because when you're full you can learn better. I think that a lot of kids did go hungry before the lunch program started, and weren't learning properly.

I think if jobs paid more, then they could get paid more, and if things didn't cost as much but you got paid more for what you did, then people wouldn't be as poor. If there were more jobs then people wouldn't be poor. If people didn't get kicked out of homes. I don't think rent should go up and down like it does. I

This picture is when my mom didn't have money and we couldn't afford to buy food, so we had to try to live without much food in the fridge. There was hardly any clothes to wear, and we couldn't buy any and we had to wear the same clothes for a couple of days. I felt so sad and embarrassed when I went to school. I was afraid that kids would make fun of me. My mom was full of stress, she would sometimes cry at night thinking about the rent and if we didn't have the money to pay the rent that we might have to move somewhere else. At night I would cry as well because I would be hungry for food.

Chris, age twelve

think rent should be, like, for a house that has, say, three bedrooms, a bathroom, living room, and stuff like that, it should only be about fifty dollars a month, because that would be good for poor people.

My goals for the future are also to help a lot of poor people, and give a lot of my food to the poor, and give some of my money to the poor because I want to be rich when I grow up, and give to the poor.

When I'm older I want to go to university and I want to become a lawyer and a part-time writer. I like to do track and field, swimming, jazz, skating, piano.

Did you learn about poverty and the reasons for it in school?

No, not at all. Never in school have they ever even mentioned poor people . . . I've never studied it once. I learned from TV, books, family talks, and I think I do know some people who are poor.

Hans

Hans, age five. His family lives below the poverty line, and as I spoke to him, he suddenly had this idea about money and where it came from. He was so excited to think he could solve his family's money problems.

❖

Where do you think money comes from?

The food bank . . . the food bank. That's where money comes from. My mom doesn't know that money comes from the food bank. I'm gonna tell her. I'm gonna show her. I'm gonna show her where money comes from. She hasn't got much money. She doesn't know it comes from the food bank. I'll show her. Then she'll smile and be happy.

Robert

Robert, age four. His family lives below the poverty line.

❖

Why are some kids poor?

Cause they don't have any money, cause they can't buy anything. Money comes from the bank, cause they have to have some from the bank.

What do you do with money?

Buy things with it, like popsicles, ice cream, . . . popsicles.

What do you get when you go to the food bank?

Cookies . . . supper!

Brian and Jennifer

Brian, age eight, and his sister Jennifer, almost three. Their family lives just above the poverty line.

❖

What does being poor mean?

BRIAN: When you don't have any money and you can't get a house and you don't have any food. I'm not poor because I have a house and I have food.

People are poor when they can't find a job or they don't have any money to buy food. Children would be poor if their mom and dad have no money.

I haven't read any books about children being poor.

What do we use money for?

JENNIFER: Treats, candy, toys, dresses, clothes, pretty shoes.

Eileen, Christina, and Jessie

Eileen, six, Christina, five, and Jessie, three, are sisters. They live way below the poverty line.

❖

What does being poor mean?

EILEEN: Not having so much money . . . you can't buy very many things . . . flowers, a camera if you want to take some pictures.

If I had money, I would give some to the poor. We could have money if we sell our things. But then we won't have things.

CHRISTINA: Not have any money to fix my bike . . . my bike needs fixing . . . no money to go out for dinner.

What can we do about it?

You can ask them, if they've got a lot of money, if they're so rich, if they could give some money.

What do we use money for?

JESSIE: We get poor, we lost the money and we get poor. Then the policeman finds the money. The policeman keeps the money.

So how are you going to get money?
From the bank.
What would you do if you had a bunch of money?
Give some to the poor.
What does poor mean?
They give the money to policeman . . .

Shaune

Shaune is almost twelve. His aunt brought him swimming with myself and another friend. While we were playing ball in the water, I talked to Shaune. It was unexpected. It had started early when he pointed to a man who was obviously homeless and said, "That's a bum and that's what I'm going to be." This surprised all three of us.

❖

Shaune said, "I'm going to get rich, then buy a Ferrari, then I'll quit my job and be a bum and live in my car. I'll eat out of the garbage and I won't wash."

What do you think being poor means?
Lots of spiders on spiderwebs.

Bill, age four

Don't you want a girlfriend or to have children someday?

No, definitely not. I want to be a bum.

Why are people poor?

They don't get good marks in school.

How can we change things?

The three R's. Recycle . . . reuse . . . and reduce.

Shaune's aunt said, "You know, his mother works and his father's a 'bum'."

Jennifer

Jennifer, age nine. It was difficult for her to talk. She spoke very quietly in small bunches of words. Jennifer lives in a group home.

❖

Once I ran away with Patty.

Being poor means not a lot of money. Working for money. Not good to be poor. Not fun.

How do poor children feel in school?

Left out sometimes. Sad, angry. I don't like school. It's hard. Sometimes there are snobs. Sometimes when you go to school, teachers are pretty mean. The last time I liked school was Grade 2 . . . good teacher . . . nice. She understands. I liked her.

What would you like to change if you had the power?

Make everyone not poor. Give food to children. Street kids – give them a place to stay, their choice. Food, nice home, clean beds . . . allowance.

How could you change school?

I could tell the teacher I'm feeling sad. I don't know if she would understand.

These two guys stole my mom's money. They threw me on the bed and did stuff to me. They hurt me. They heard my mom coming and they tried to stuff me in a big suitcase. They told me to shut up, don't tell. They said tell your mother you fell down. I was five. It lasted about two years. When we were in a transition house, I told . . . they called the cops. One guy got arrested . . . I think he got a year or two. I don't know. My goals are to have a nice home. A lot of children. And I will take good care of them.

One day this girl was poor and had no money. Her house was a mess and empty and she only had a little bit of food. She slept on a mat upstairs. This girl came up to her and gave her $10 cause she was poor. The girl felt happy. She went to the store and bought a chair and food that was cereal and Kraft Dinner, mushroom soup, and cool-aid and she bought glasses.

Rhonda, age seven

Sophia

Sophia, age three.

Do you know what not having money means?

You don't have money to buy a popsicle. Sometimes my mom gives me money. If she don't have money, then she can't buy me a popsicle. If you don't have money and you just take it and not pay for it, that means you're like stealing it . . .

Nicky

Nicky, age sixteen. This was given to me by End Legislated Poverty.

❖

As a young person just starting out on minimum wage, I had no idea what I was up against. Working full time just to pay rent and barely eat is frustrating. When you have no money and you're stuck cashing in empty pop bottles just for bus fare you begin to wonder why you even do it to begin with? I'm not making ends meet and not being able to save for luxuries. A luxury to me is opening my fridge and finding milk there when I want it. A single person in British Columbia working full time on minimum wage is still over $3000 below the poverty line. People at the bottom of the poverty level are tired of struggling and still not making ends meet. In order to stop poverty we need

This is a happy home because they have a dad.

Lana, age six

to raise minimum wage to $8.26 an hour and lower housing costs. Since I'm under eighteen, I receive fifty cents less per hour than an adult but yet I still pay rent and government taxes. Equal minimum wage should be given to every man, woman, and child. Age discrimination must stop. It's time our government took a serious look at where our economy is headed. People at the bottom of the poverty scale need to benefit and succeed also!

Barbara

Barbara is only thirteen, but knows a lot about life out on the street. I have known about her for a long time. She was living in a shelter in my last book, because her family couldn't find housing. That's when rents were rising so high and there were few vacancies, especially for families on welfare. I have wanted to interview her for a long time. Today her parent phoned and said that Barbara wanted to talk to me for the book on children. I interviewed her by phone.

❖

I'm busy. You know I have to go out. I only have about five minutes to talk with you. Are you gonna make me tell you everything [angrily], are you?

No. I have a rule that children only tell me what they choose to tell me, and they can change their name and nobody knows who they are.

Well I want to use my own name.

But that may embarrass you later on.

I don't give a shit. I don't care . . . I don't care . . . I don't care.

What things would you like to change if you had the power?

You are asking me that? Well, I'd change the school, the teachers . . . they should be more helpful. They say if you need help, ask, but some kids are too embarrassed to ask. If you can't do it, they say do it again. They should know you need help. They should offer it. Instead, they just get mad and tell you to do it and you can't. Teachers should pay more attention instead of paying attention to making money. They are more interested in the money they make than us.

I had one good teacher; he was a special, nice man. He didn't give you attention just because you were poor; he treated everyone the same. Everyone got five dollars on their birthday. Once my tooth came out. This teacher was in Grade 5. Anyway, he said, let me see that tooth. When I wasn't looking, he must have thrown that tooth in the garbage. Instead he handed me an envelope that was sealed. He told me to put it under my pillow and that the tooth fairy would leave some money. Anyway, he must have put a twenty-dollar bill in the envelope because that's what was there in the morning. He was kind. He was a nice man. I was only in his class for two months because I moved out of the province.

Teachers pay too much attention to kids that are poor. They don't treat them the same as everybody else. One teacher brought a lamp and some curtains to my house. I was so embarrassed, I hated it, but my mom was pleased. I don't like anyone to know that I'm on welfare. It embarrasses me. Kids in school make fun of kids that are on welfare. They call them names. I'm in an alternative school now. I like it. No one knows I'm on welfare. I don't tell them.

I was told that you have lived on the street for a while?

I never once slept out on the street. I didn't sleep at home. I slept at different friends' houses, but I never stayed more than three days at anyone's house. I never wore my welcome out.

I understand you are clean now. Congratulations!

I've been clean for two months. I had a slip, like these friends, really close friends, friends that I didn't expect to, offered me stuff and I took it, but I am clean for two months. I was doing pot and acid. I did acid once in a while, it was great . . .

Don't you have flashbacks?

Yeah, but they are great. I enjoy them. They are fun. It's just like doing acid, like you just relive it. It's great.

Most of the kids in my alternative school are in group homes. I'm one of the only ones living at home. I've been home for two months. My goal is to be an accountant some day.

I guess you would have to stay clean?

God no! They do it – all those kind of people do it – on weekends. I know accountants that do it, but they just do it on weekends. I know I would have to stay in school, graduate, go to Vancouver Community College, then take a business course. That would probably take till I'm 25. Until then I want a career as a singer. I'm a good singer, really good.

Are you going to counselling?

No, I don't trust my counsellor. She said I could tell her anything, that it was confidential. I told her about a fight I had. It was supposed to be confidential. When I saw my social worker, she knew all about it. She started to question me, making a big thing about it. My mom never told her, so it has to be the counsellor. I don't trust her. I'm not going back. Anyway, I've gotta go. Friends are waiting for me.

This is my family: my mom, dad and me. We are poor because the government took all of our money, because he is greedy. My house has a TV but not much else. We don't have much money to buy clothes, to get groceries so we had to go to my dad's mom and dad's place to eat. We feel sad.

Robin, age eight

Maybe I can see you around sometime and talk some more?
Sure.

❖

(I tried to see her later, but she had been gone for a few days. Her family and friends really love her and are trying to get her off the street.)

Tammy

Tammy, age seventeen.

❖

Why do you think people are poor?

It has a lot to do with the system, the government, the welfare system.

I'm pregnant. I had my first son when I was sixteen. He's in foster care. I'm determined to get him back. I'll be having my baby in July or August. It's kind of nerve wracking because I don't know if I'm going to be getting my first boy back.

I've got a bad heart – it could have been because, when I was younger, five or six years old, I had scarlet fever. I almost died and I had heart palpitations. That could be coming out now that I'm pregnant again.

I've been on the street since I was fifteen years old, sometimes at home, and in and out of group homes. I'm just coming to terms with it now. I'm getting things in my life straightened out, just starting to get problems to do with my past all together. Now I'm living in an apartment building, I'm living on my own and I've got a cat and I'm finding it hard to cope, having my place alone. I'm used to being around people. I've got a lot of friends – so-called friends – down here. My street family consists of several people, I've got two sets of dads, two sets of moms, fifteen street sisters, about twenty street brothers, and basically what I did on the street was I'd sell drugs. I don't say that pushing drugs is any way of quote, unquote, getting rich. It's no good. You're hurting other people, and I haven't done drugs and I haven't drank since December. I stopped about a month into my pregnancy. It's very hard with peer pressure like, but it's getting easier and easier. My dreams are having a big family, having a job, and being totally away from down here. There's a good chance. I'm going to school here. I've got a job lined up for when I get my diploma, and it's coming true for me now, but I don't live down here, I'm not a part of the scene down here anymore. I still come down here to say hello sometimes, but my life isn't wrapped up in down here anymore.

When I first came on the street I was fifteen, I would stay with friends. Living on the street consisted of several things for me, like dealing drugs, I worked, I was a prostitute, B&Es, auto theft, panhandling. Just a whole bunch of different things. I felt terrible inside. I said to myself, I don't care what happens. It's my life. I'm gonna make it or break it and I broke it. Like, now I come to think about it, it's not worth it, the pain and suffering, to go through what I went through. It's really lonely, you want to belong so much. You want to be in the crowd so much, you'll do anything. My gut says kids should realize that they're not going to make a life . . .

But who's going to make them realize?

Well, one of my dreams is getting a house, and like helping the street kids clean up, help them get jobs, give them a guiding path . . . say, hey, I know what you're going through. I went through the same thing. It would take a person who was a street kid to help a street kid . . . or a person that lived on the streets that knows what it's like to guide them through it, get them off of it. That's what's really needed for street kids. The street is not glamorous like a lot of kids think it is. You always have to watch your back because you never know, you've got the police on your tail for prostitution, B&Es, auto theft, selling dope, all that. You always have something in the back of your head saying, this is not right, it's not all glamorous, I'm hurting other people as well as myself.

When I first came on the street, I thought it would be great, I don't have to listen to anybody. I don't have to live under anybody's roof. As a kid I had a really rough life. My mom and dad divorced when I was six. I was moved from one place to another, never had a steady life. I was sexually abused when I was five years old, emotionally and verbally abused by my mother.

Then it got to the point it got physical. And I guess I said, hey, if I go out into the street I don't have to listen to nobody. Nobody will tell me what to do and that's what led to it all . . .

Street kids need that guidance and support, not just from one person but several people in a group that lived on the street. I never had a pimp. I've had people came up to me and say, hey, you wanna work for me? I go, no, I want the money for myself, not for you. Now I've got a little boy and another baby on the way. Just think, last year or the year before that I was on the street, partying and partying, drunk every day, stoned every day. I look back and I laugh and say, that's not me. I've been dry since December.

I hope from this book that kids and people will understand that street life isn't the way to go. It's nothing but filth, crime, and disgust, and you'll regret it. I did. Being on welfare at seventeen, it's an easy way out, like you can sit and do nothing. But you don't make enough to survive. You're surviving one month to the next. It's not just money. It's . . . you need the basic support of friends and people you can rely on to help you out when you're in a bind.

Why did they apprehend your son?

They said it was poor parenting and neglect. I missed a doctor's appointment, so I'm fighting to get him back. I'm visiting him; I've got visiting rights to him. I want him back in my custody. I want him to be with me. And the social worker gave me a really good feeling today. He said, you visit your son on a regular basis, and if it works out, maybe it'll work out to more than visits. He was totally against me in the beginning. He said, I'm going to fight you getting your son back, so today he gave me new hope.

What about the new baby?

I'm keeping this one. The social worker said the only way they would apprehend this baby is if I miss doctor's appointments, neglect or abuse the baby. I will be eighteen in two months. I was sixteen when I had my first boy. I have been getting ready for the baby. I'm getting a crib, a stroller, baby clothes, changing table, bassinet. It's all being given to me. I don't have to pay anything. My apartment is quiet. It's kind of funny because when me and

The big M stands for money.

Patty, age eleven

my mom first moved into Vancouver, that's the apartment we moved into, it's the apartment I'm living in now.

❖

(I met Tammy again in October. She looked sad. She said, "I had my baby, but the baby was apprehended. They said neglect but it's not true." I didn't bombard her with questions, just suggested she make sure she has a lawyer.)

Patty

Patty, age eleven. She is bright, intelligent, street-wise, and extremely articulate.

❖

What does being poor mean?

Not having any money. Not having a place to stay. Living on the street. Being on welfare. Not having a very good job. Living in a dump.

Have you ever been homeless?

When I first moved – I'm originally from Ontario – when I first moved to Vancouver, we didn't have a place to stay for a couple of days, so we stayed at a family shelter. Which wasn't very fun. But we stuck to it for a couple of days. Then we found a place. We lived there for a while – we stayed there for about a year or maybe more, and then we went back into the shelter, for eight months, till my sister got us kicked out by throwing a tantrum or having a nervous breakdown or something. So then we had to stay at another shelter for a couple of months, and then we moved to a house. It wasn't a very good house but it was okay. It didn't have any mice or anything, but it was pretty creepy. Then we moved out to another shelter for homeless people . . . and then we moved to a really big dump. Then we moved to Ontario Street, and now we live in Burnaby.

Are you out of school right now?

Well, not really. I'm just not going . . .

Why?

I just don't feel like it. Well, I just need some time off. I'm in grade five. I can do the work if I feel like it. It's not hard. The math's really easy. I plan to go back tomorrow.

At the moment I'm living in a group home, but I haven't been there for a few weeks. I've been, not really on the street. Most of the time I've been with my mom or hanging out down here . . . or I'd be at my friends'.

If you could go back in time, what would have made your life easier?

Well, I thought it was pretty easy before we moved here but then, when we moved here things started to get rough, and everything started to go down the drain at first and then we started to build up.

Do you think you're in danger of becoming a street person?

Well yes, sometimes, because I'm not home very often. I'm not at my group home very often. I hang out down here all the time.

What would it take to change your lifestyle?

It would take a lot. I need to think about that.

I survive by watching people around me, see how they do it. I don't like to hang out down here by myself at night, so if I'm by myself down here at night time, then I'll stay here until one of my friends is leaving, then I'll leave. I'll go to a friend's.

If you had the power, what would you do about poverty?

I'd move all the rich people onto the street, and all the poor people into the rich houses, and let the rich people see how it feels to be poor. I'd also make a job increase, which means more jobs, so that people have less chance of being poor. I'd have schools, pre-schools – schools that are good, that teach children how to read and write. What they need is love . . . and some attention. But children are not like a toy where you could pick it up and put it down whenever you want. Like a video game, or a

Patty, age eleven

tape, a music tape, you stop it wherever you want. Life is not like that.

My sister's on the street. She's twelve and she's living on the street. She does drugs. She has a pretty messy life. I would hate to see myself looking like that. I'd hate to be in her shoes.

How did she start being like that?

She feels – this is just a guess – that the only way to make people pay attention to her is to make them worry, I mean constantly pay attention to her. I worry about her. Nobody really does anything. My mom, she worries but my mom knows she can't do anything about it. The authorities won't do anything about it. My mom's tried picking her up. She'll just take off again. I have no idea what's going to happen to her. I see her often. She'll come home at the beginning of the month, get bus fare, food, clothes, and money, and then she'll take off again.

Street kids need more places where they can go to . . . like community centres and places that they know that they'll be safe if they have to take off somewhere . . . they can go down there and not get busted. Even rich people have street kids. I think we should get a new government, a better government. If we had a better government, we wouldn't have to worry about street kids, people living on the street, and stuff like that. Less crime.

How do you avoid drugs and pimps?

To tell you the truth, I don't like drinking. I don't like the taste of beer or any shit like that. Smoking, well, it's okay sometimes. I don't do drugs. I never have and never will. As far as it goes for pimps, so far, if somebody comes up to me and starts talking to me like that, I tell them to fuck off.

Sylvia

Sylvia, age fifteen, is a young person with Down's syndrome. She has a large extended family that loves her very much. Her family, in spite of past poverty, has encouraged her to achieve as much as she can. She gives so much love to all who know her, including me.

❖

I'm in school. I'm in junior high. I like to do art in my spare time and crafts with my teacher. I have had work training, and I do lots of stuff there. I am fifteen.

Why do you think people are poor?

Because they don't have any food or money. They don't have any jobs. They don't have any houses. They don't have any friends to play with.

I was poor before with my mother. It was kind of different. I was left with no money. Now I have six dollars in the bank. I used to feel really mad and sad. I didn't have as much as other kids and they cheated on me.

My mom didn't have any money because she didn't go to work. Now she does and I get a school allowance and I feel good about it.

Poor people need money. People need money to get food.

The poor people live in boxes.

Last time my cousin said she saw a restaurant and the name of the restaurant was Richard's and she went inside and she bought take-out food and she gave it to the poor people. That night I dreamed that was me what she did and I started to cry.

Julie, age unknown

What are your dreams for the future?

I dream about art, and crafts with paint and felts. I went to the peace march with my mom. I like doing anti-poverty work with my mom. I like drawing stuff at her office. I like being with people and I like being with my friends. I'd like to work with my mother at anti-poverty stuff.

Graham

Graham, age thirteen, comes from a family where there is one wage-earner who works two jobs. In spite of that, they are still living below the poverty line.

❖

Being poor is no money to buy things like your friends have. Living in poor surroundings, scavenging through garbage . . . not much food . . . not much fruit. Poor kids feel embarrassed. They don't tell anyone in school. They feel sad and frustrated, but happy to have friends. They don't want to ruin it so they don't tell their friends. Some poor kids get into drugs with a dealer and make money for their family. If you are poor, you can shoplift . . . if you have to. If they are big, they can jump people. Do you know what that means? It means jump on them and rip off their jacket if it is an expensive one, and sell it for food or drugs or something.

The girl is sad because she has no clothes and her house is empty. Not much food or furniture. Her friends have nice clothes.

Louise, age eight-and-a-half

Teachers should treat kids more equal. Teachers treat poor kids badly.

What do you think are some solutions?

Join up with the community and help them out, distribute food. Kids could bring stuff they don't use to school, and kids could take what they needed. Supply meals. There should be more housing for poor families. The government should give good paying jobs so people could pay for their housing. The jobs should be near the housing. People should have more understanding. There should be a market where people who are poor could pick out the food they needed for free. Finally, give them a chance. Help them join into society so that they are not alone.

Paul

Paul, age sixteen. I've known Paul since he was three years old. He and his family have always lived way below the poverty line.

❖

Why are people poor?

It's hard to say. There's too many people, there's not enough food to go around. I don't know, it's the way the world is. It's hard. I don't know, it's life. There's lots of charity, but charities got limits too, right? Everything's got a limit to it. There's more people than there is charity, you know. It's hard. At school once they called me Welfare Pauley. I got into a fight with another kid in my class. It wasn't too serious, the fight, but it was basically standing up for myself.

Solutions? Better living conditions is one thing. There's still a lot of old hotels down here. The more low-cost housing, I guess, the better for a lot of people, you know. Hotels are not safe. People are getting killed all the time. You gotta second thought on everything, you know, while you're walking down the street, anything can happen, anything's possible, you know? You can die any time.

If I'd had more money as a kid, it's hard to say what I would've used it on. Probably do what a lot of other people do, share it a bit. I would have changed a lot of things in my life. I would have made sure I would have had a house to live in as long as I'm on this planet, and the family and stuff. I would have taken a course for a recording engineer.

Do you think you still have a chance of doing that?

Oh yeah, but I've got to save up the money, it's quite a bit. I'm not in school. Yeah, I finished in Grade 8. I plan to go back eventually. Yeah, yeah, I quit because I just couldn't stand the hassle from the counsellors and stuff, you know. They were picking on me because I was a kid with the less money. They figured, they accused me of being on drugs and all kind of things which I was not.

I was about seven when I first knew I was poor. Basically, the way everything felt around me, you know. Not having a lot of money, a lot of the kids have a lot more than you have. You just got to put up with it, you know? That's what I did. Yeah.

I've lived in quite a few places in my life, between the age I am now and when I was really young. Even when I was first born we moved a couple of times between that and the time I was three years old. That's how it's been. I didn't pay a lot of attention to the fact of moving; that's something I never thought a lot about, but you get used to it after awhile, you know. Changing schools and moving to other places. It's hard to get to know new people, you know. All the new kids, you gotta find out who you want to be friends with and who you don't, who's gonna be a real friend to you and who's not.

I've lived in one house where I felt unsafe, in the Mount Pleasant area. There's a lot going on there, just a bad neighbourhood basically.

My plans for the future are to take the recording course, take both levels of that and eventually, when I get the money together, open up my own studio.

How will you get the money together?

Like I said, I'm gonna try to get a job. The only thing you can really get is McDonald's. Minimum wage usually, five-fifty to six bucks. That's all it is. It's quite low. I don't know if it has a medicare plan or dental. I don't think so. I had a job before, helping out a friend with his paper route and that. It was not too bad, was kind of fun, and now I'm a musician right now. I'm employed as a musician. I play mainly rock and blues and stuff like that . . .

(I spoke with Paul again in September.)

What's been happening over the summer?

I went for three vacations, a couple close by. My grandfather died this summer, and a lot of bad luck. Still looking for a job. I do volunteer work. I'm still looking for a full-time job.

Would you think about going back to school?

No, I don't think so.

Have your goals changed?

My goals now? Well, there's a few new ones. I want to get into a new group, like a new band. I'm not in a band at this time. I want to pull it together and start playing clubs and that . . . you know? Get some money together that way.

What do you think your chances are of making it in the music world?

Very slim. There's too much competition. It's very competitive, you know.

What is the job scene like out there for you?

For most people my age it's mostly Burger King or McDonald's. I think student wage is maybe six dollars an hour. It's not a lot, but it's passable, I guess. I've just filled out an application, but I haven't taken it back in yet.

That's not what you really want to do, is it?

No. I want to be a musician, record producer, recording engineer, songwriter . . . that's what I'm already doing. I'm a songwriter and a musician now, but I want to do that for a living. I want to be a recording engineer. It would be great, but it costs money. I'm not too sure if I could get a grant. It could be possible.

I'm looking towards the future, I don't think about the past too much anymore. Well, at this point it looks like it's gonna happen. The present is rough.

How do you manage to stay off drugs when you are around them all the time?

I just never wanted to do that. I'm scared of it, that's why. The fear of it. If I would've done that, I realize what I could have lost. I could have lost everything that I have.

How did you manage to say no when you were offered drugs?

Daisy, age ten

You just gotta be forceful about it. Sometimes it comes to the point when you have to tell them, tell them straight. It comes to a point when you might get into a fight over it, but I still say no, no. You gotta stick to your guns.

❖

(A month later I saw Paul again. He said he was playing guitar in a group out in Coquitlam.)

Kate

Kate is sixteen, full of fun, and great to be with. She is from a low-income family.

❖

When I was twelve, thirteen, I missed a lot of school. I just didn't go. My stepfather was abusive to me. One night, it was midnight, I was at a friend's house. I was putting my shoes on to go home. He found me. He pulled me by the hair. He punched me. I told him to eff off. One time when I was fifteen I had my leg over the couch; he started to punch and hit me so I kicked him in the face four times and he hasn't touched me since.

When I ran away, I would stay at a friend's house here and a friend's house there. Once when I was fourteen I ran away, but my parents found me. They told me they would send for the police if I didn't come home, so I went home.

When I was fifteen I moved in with two girls and three guys. We lived in New Westminster. The guys were nineteen and seventeen and fifteen and the girls were fifteen.

I was smart enough not to get into hooking. I shoplifted instead, or I would go home for a day and steal from my mother or grandmother or uncle. I was doing pot, coke, heroin. We all were.

Like you steal some jewelry and sell it on the street. I got caught once stealing red hair dye. The others snatched an older person's purse. I was against it. I didn't like it – that person had done no harm. They shouldn't have done that.

How did you get off drugs?

I just went off them. I have been off them for eight months.

I'm living at home. I called lots of places. I was motivated. I called the youth pre-employment. I wanted a job. I made lots of calls. I called Gordon House Youth Works and they said come on down. They accepted me, but first they asked me if I could work with different races of people. I didn't have any problems working with street people because they were all my friends. We hang out near the Capitol Six on Granville. Seven of us are working. Not everyone is clean yet. I worked for Western Canada Wilderness for a while. It was part time. This job is better – it's full time. Some stores are giving kids a chance and hiring them through this program. They are getting a chance, getting experience. It has really helped me motivate myself into school again.

My goals are to work up to Grade 12, get a part-time job (I'm working and paying room and board now, you know). Go to college, maybe work with latchkey kids. Maybe even be a teacher. I have a younger brother and sister. I want to keep them off the street. I have another sister in Toronto.

You know, most of the street kids I know don't associate with

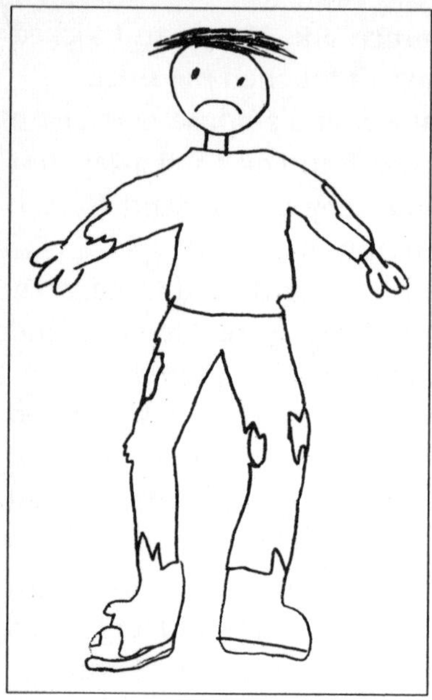

I wish I could go to Australia to see the kangaroos but my mom can't afford it.

I wish that I could have more toys but mom has to wait for more money.

My mom gets angry that she doesn't have enough money.

This is a poor person who doesn't have a home or any money. His clothes are ripped. He feels sad.

Lyle, age seven-and-a-half

their parents, so everybody down on Granville is one big, happy family. I go there as much as I can. They are my friends.

How do you think we can help street kids?

More programs like Gordon House. Higher pay. $5.50 is not enough because some kids work part time. We need more people working on the street that have been on the street and become clean. They should work with the street kids and share with them, tell them their stories and what happened to them, but it should be fun, not lecturing. Change the attitude of the people that work near Granville. They think they are so high and mighty and they don't give a shit about us because they make so much money a year. They just don't care. They say, get a job, get a job . . . First you have to help motivate someone, then give them a chance, give them a chance.

Steven

Steven, age fourteen. This was the keynote speech at the Surrey Child Poverty Forum in April 1989.

❖

Hi, my name is Steven and I'm here to talk about children living in poverty in Surrey. I have a first-hand knowledge of this subject because I have been living in poverty for twelve years and I'm fourteen now.

I'm just going to give you some examples of what it's like to be poor. I live in a housing co-op that is in a richer area of Surrey. The more well-off kids call it "the Ghetto" and the kids that live in it are called "Co-op Kids" and it is not very pleasant.

When some of the kids in my class are going to a movie and ask me if I want to come, I have to say no because my mom doesn't have enough money. That makes me feel deprived.

Me and my mom get into fights quite often because of money. I ask to borrow some money and she does not have enough to lend me. It makes me angry not to be able to get money when I ask to borrow it. My friends who are not poor don't even have to ask for money. Their parents give it to them, and that makes me jealous.

I cannot afford all the designer clothes that are worn by my fellow classmates. We shop at Value Village and those clothes are used and sometimes stained and ripped, and that makes me feel like dirt. Two years ago, our school was putting on a circus for the parents and my teacher sent me home with a note, asking my mom to send me to school as a hobo because he knew I couldn't afford a fancy costume like the rest of the kids, and that was so degrading I just decided I couldn't go to school or the circus.

Before we joined our food co-op, Kraft Dinner used to be our main diet for supper, as well as beef liver and hamburger. We had lots of days where we just ate potatoes. We can't afford juice and most of the time I feel hungry because there is not a large enough selection of food in our house and I have to eat toast and crackers to keep feeling full. I can't invite my friends for dinner because we can only afford to have soup or one thing like salad, and the kids usually have soup, salad, and a main course with meat, and dessert.

I hope the politicians are watching this so they can raise the minimum wage and welfare rates so people like me can live better than I do now. And if they could make more jobs that were not degrading, like an adult working at McDonald's. Eliminate poverty all together.

Tina

Tina, age eighteen.

❖

Why am I poor? Because my job doesn't pay me enough to live on. I work at McDonald's, but it's always part time. I never make full time, so I don't get any benefits or job security.

When I went to school I quit in Grade 9. I went to work, but after the summer I was laid off. I would like employers to be made to be more responsible, and not be allowed to use workers, then throw them away like garbage.

I would like to have a full-time job. I have to make my room rent. I don't want welfare. Sometimes I think about becoming a hooker. I think working for companies that keep your hours

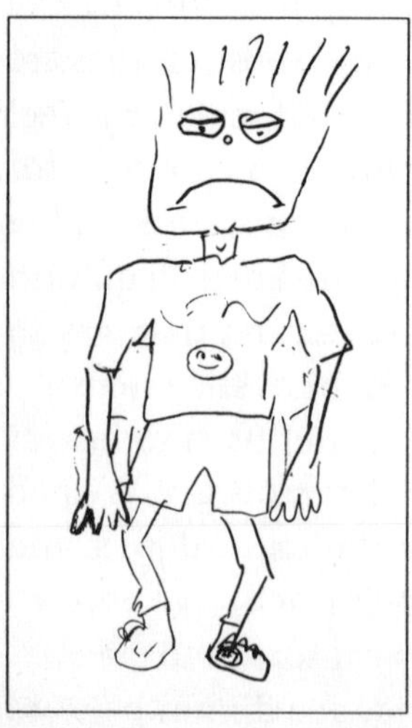

If you're poor, you're sad.
Tyler, age thirteen

down makes a woman look for a man to help her. I've got a boyfriend. He helps with the rent. He pushes me around when he's high. He really beat me up last Christmas. If I had a good job with a pay that I could live on, maybe I could leave him. I don't know. Maybe I'll go back to school.

If I could change things I would make it easier to go back to school. I would make these outfits pay a wage that people could live on. I would give every poor person a dentist and medicine. My teeth are bad! I would make bus fare cheaper. It costs so much to go to work. Like, if I only get four hours work and I have to pay bus fare, it's hard. I'd make rich people have to give some of their money to the poor.

(from *No Way to Live*)

Andrea

Andrea is in her late teens. I talked with her in the Ovaltine Café on Hastings. She came to Vancouver when she ran away from home. Her father had been having sex with her since she was ten. She hated him, so took off and hitchhiked here. Sometimes she had to give sex for a meal or for a ride. People who she asked to help her just wanted to send her back to her father. She thought that no one believed her. Her mother didn't.

❖

I survived. I've got a job and a boyfriend now. It's not too bad except when he drinks he gets real mad and I get scared of him. He's hit me a few times . . . It could be worse . . . At least I'm not hooking. When I came here and I had no place to sleep I couldn't go for help because they would have sent me back. So I'd pick up a man if he had a place. Then I'd go home with him. It was safer than being on the streets. Of course I'd have to let them do what they wanted to my body. That's the price of a place to stay isn't it? One guy brought his friends back to the room and they took turns using my body . . . There was nothing I could do . . . It was real nasty.

It's better now though. I'm nineteen and there's no fucking way they can send me back. I work as a waitress down the street.

Sometimes I get pissed just to forget. Sometimes I do drugs but not much.

Homelessness is being scared to go home . . . Homelessness is having to have sex for a place to sleep . . . Homelessness is no one caring about you, like not belonging anywhere . . . I think I'm pregnant. I know my baby would love me . . . But my boyfriend's not too happy about it.

(from *Under the Viaduct*)

Anna

Anna was living in a downtown Vancouver hotel room with her mother and sister. She is a beautiful, gentle-looking girl with long black hair and big brown eyes. I asked her if I could talk to her about homelessness. She was very shy.

❖

Homeless is having no food . . . and no furniture . . . A home should have food and furniture.

When I come home from school I just go to my room and listen to my radio. It's so boring, nothing to do but sit in the room. No food, just water to drink. There's so many cockroaches. I don't let anyone in school know where I live . . . We eat at the 44 [the Evelyne Saller Centre, a downtown drop-in centre with an inexpensive cafeteria] . . . I'm not in school today, I just couldn't make it.

Carol, Anna's mother, said Anna had missed a lot of school.

To look at Anna you would see a clean, neatly dressed, beautiful young girl who could be from Point Grey. She wouldn't be a homeless statistic, she wouldn't be visibly homeless.

I wanted to hug her. I wanted to make everything okay for her. I wanted her to finish school. She's in Grade 10. I wanted her to have a fair chance. I know what she is up against.

This is another story that doesn't have an ending.

I never met the younger teenager. One thing though, the most important thing, there was obviously love there; Carol loved her kids.

(from *Under the Viaduct*)

When I first came to this school I was poor because my mom lost her job and she got a new job as a post lady. I felt sad because people call me names and I met a friend named Christie.

Cindy, age eleven

When I was in the 4th grade I had a friend named Cindy who didn't have money. Everybody would call her names and she needed a friend so me and Amanda would help her at recess and lunch. Everyone would call her names like lice head, stealer, you are poor, and make her feel very sad, but she was glad she had two good friends, me and Amanda, and she was very thankful to us because we helped her out.

Christie, age ten-and-a-half

Adults Who Were Poor as Children

Danny

Danny is a young man, intelligent, bright, and capable, who could easily do well in any profession he chose. In his early school years, his family lived below the poverty line.

I don't remember much about school. I didn't like it. There was one teacher, one teacher, she had long red fingernails, yeah, long red fingernails. She was a bitch. She kept saying to me, "You are pathetic . . . you are pathetic . . . " I don't know why. I don't know why she said that. She had these long red fingernails, she was a bitch, and she kept telling me I was pathetic.

Would you think of taking some adult education courses?

(angrily) No, no.

Renee

A friend gave me Renee's number. She has a three-year-old daughter who was going to do some sketches for me. Renee said she used to be a hooker. I asked her if she would agree to an interview. She said sure.

I came from a small town in Québec. We were not poor, we always had food. I was the eighth child. A previous child of my mother had died of leukemia. My mother had some kind of

If you leave home and think your parents hate you – well it's your funeral.

Graham, age thirteen

nervous breakdown and couldn't take care of me. It was always that way. When I was in Grade 7, my father's friend took me in the forest and fondled me. I told my father. A few days later my father got drunk and beat up the man. My mother blamed me and said it was my fault. That it was normal for a man to fondle me. That that's the way it was. I think it had happened to her as a child and she had learned just to accept it, and she wanted me to do the same. In Grade 2 I ran away with a boy for twenty-four hours. We made a bed in a field.

When I was twelve, I used to talk to this man. He was about fifty. I wasn't happy at home. He told me to come and live with him, that no one would ever find me. I was so trusting and innocent. I went home to pack some clothes. I left with six bags, but my mother saw me. She screamed, Renee where are you going? You know, I know now what that guy was up to. I didn't know then.

I started turning tricks when I was sixteen, with teachers, psychologists, for cigarettes, for pinball games, for skipping class. I had a friend who did it with me. She was tougher than me. She has three massage parlours now. At sixteen they thought I was going into Montreal for a hair-dressing class but I was hanging out on the streets.

When I was eighteen, I was living with a forty-year-old biker/pusher. I was doing tricks and he was dealing. We were like Bonnie and Clyde. After, I learned to keep my own money.

I met some women who were doing the bad trick sheet. They told me I was strong and wise. They were feminist. They helped me see the powerlessness of hooking. I stopped one year later, got pregnant, and now have a three-year-old daughter. It's been hard relocating in Vancouver, but I'm going to school and I go to the food bank. It's really hard, but I'll never go back to hooking again. I love my daughter. I had a one-night stand, that I connived to get pregnant. My family has disowned me, but I have some good friends here in Vancouver.

Roy

Roy is in his early thirties. He says his childhood poverty has left him with poor self esteem.

❖

It wasn't so much grinding poverty; we were never really

What do you think being poor means?
A house with cracks in the walls.

Lana, age six

desperately poor. I was walking around a couple of evenings ago and I noticed parents taking their kids to the S.A. [Salvation Army] for junk clothes. I never had that problem. My problem was more sort of a resignation to . . . Basically, my mother was the bread-winner in the family, like, my father ended up being close to another kid. She probably could have claimed him as a dependent on her income tax.

My mother worked in a laundry, very low pay, very very poorly paid. She was at one time making 95 cents an hour . . . there was just me, my mom, and my father. You see, my father was sort of an itinerant worker. Sometimes he'd work and he could make lots of money. There was a couple times he'd go up north and come back with oodles and boodles of money, but he had no sense of control – it was sort of boom, bust, sort of the way Canada is – boom, bust. There's money all over the place, and then suddenly there isn't that much.

Well the thing is there's a lot of violence in my family, probably due to the economics. My mother was a quite violent woman. That was spurred on by the fact that she was doing all the bread winning and this asshole father was a jerk. It affected not only education but one's whole self concept. My whole self concept ended up being destroyed because my mom didn't really show a lot of the affection or warmth that other mothers did, right. Grade 10, I went back to school and finished that. I didn't have a lot of nice things. I didn't get my first bicycle til I was nine – I didn't learn how to ride a bike til I was nine. I was the original latchkey kid – that whole phenomenon of the seventies, I was going through that ten years earlier. I was six years old and I was staying with my grandparents, and my parents wanted me, they were living in central Alberta then. My father had a job. He was working in the oilfields, cooking. They put me on a train and my parents picked me up in Calgary. I was on that train by myself [this with great sadness] . . . From eight, nine, I basically got up, and the thing is, I did all my stuff – I dressed myself, washed myself, made toast and milk for breakfast. I thought that was just the way things normally were. It wasn't until some time later that I found, when I was talking to a friend who has a kid that is older than I was when I did the train trip . . . He said, "I wouldn't let

If your on the streets on your own your likely to come across Drugs.
Graham, age thirteen

my son ride the bus downtown alone, let alone on a train to Calgary." It sort of had a terrible effect on my self esteem and my sense of self confidence because when a kid is really poor, he's not brought up with the illusion and the sense of reality that middle-class kids and upper-class kids are that, well, they have money and they can go out and do things that poor kids can't, and they can develop skills that poor kids can't. The thing is, it wasn't until I was 20 that I discovered I was really a fucked-up person. I took a trip for the first time in my life. Just jumped out on the road and hitchhiked a long way. I was on the road for a month and a half. But the thing is, I sort of discovered, when I got down the road, that, I realized, my Christ, I just didn't know how – unless I had to see someone for something – I really couldn't survive. I was on welfare for a year and a half before an LIP grant [Local Initiatives Program] came and saved me.

Stella

Stella is a quiet, shy person. Her outward appearance shows no signs of the tough life she has experienced. I don't really know how she feels inwardly. She just told me her story.

❖

I can't remember, really, if I was poor or not before I was

sixteen. Anyway, I had run away. I went to Owen Sound – that's north of Toronto, it's a holiday area – to get a job, but the season hadn't started. I had no experience. I couldn't get a job. I made friends with another girl. She was pregnant. We lived in a taxi stand and old cars. I lost my shoes and my clothes. My friend later gave up her baby, but then she became suicidal. I got involved with an undercover cop and he had me sent back to my family. I ran away three times. I lived on the street for three years. I was also in foster homes but I always ran away.

A friend and I found a neat way to survive. In Toronto, because of the cold weather, if you rented a room in winter and paid one month's rent, the landlord couldn't throw you out because you could freeze to death, so we would pay one month's rent, then stay in the room rent free til they threw us out. We kept our food in a bureau drawer. We lived mainly on peanut butter, bread, and cool-aid. We panhandled for money.

When I got pregnant, I wanted to keep my baby. I was eligible for welfare. I was eligible for rent too, so I came off the street. I guess having my baby got me off the street.

Elizabeth

Elizabeth is a young woman with two young daughters. She is alone but has a large extended family. She may go back to school to do early childhood education and work with children.

When she told her story, she looked like a little girl as she relived the pain of the abuse that she went through. She kept a strong grip on the tears and no matter how full her eyes were with pain, she never let one tear fall.

❖

I never thought of how I grew up as poor. I guess when I was about eight, nine, I didn't have the same things as all the rest of the kids. Birthday parties . . . a girl lived across the street and her dad was a police officer. We weren't invited to the party but we went over there. We didn't know they had a party. And there were all our friends, all dressed up in all these pretty little dresses, and we had on our summer dresses. Even then I didn't think of myself as poor. Mom would get her cheque and if it were more than what she thought, we would get to go out for dinner. Veal cutlets . . . to her that was expensive eating, veal cutlets. My mom, she was one strong lady. I can't think of anybody else's mom who could be stronger. She raised three boys and then she had me and my little sister. She raised all of us on her own. Bringing up three boys was hard, and then when she got two girls – we were on welfare, we didn't have always enough to make it through, but she always somehow got dresses, little tap shoes for us girls and that. Always, always dressed us very nicely.

When she passed away, she put in her will that this other family that we knew would look after us. I was ten years old; my little sister was a year younger, nine. It was just before her ninth birthday. I remember shortly after that, another girl's mother passed away in our school, and I said something to her one day and all her friends turned round and says, how can you be so mean? Her mom just died, and I stood there and went, what do you think *I* went through? I've just finished going through that. I felt really hurt. I think that was the first time that I really got hurt by my friends. My feelings had nothing to do with it. This other girl whose family had a bit more than me was worth more, could *feel* more, because I didn't have so much.

My mother died of cancer. My dad left when I was just two years old, after my sister was born. When my mother died my brothers were sixteen, nineteen, and twenty. We stayed for a year with this other family. They had a problem child in their home and, maybe it was just me, but I've talked to my little sister – everything that went wrong was *my* fault. She'll say so now, but then she wouldn't. So they decided, well, we don't need another problem child; we'll get rid of her. We'll adopt the little one. She was ten then, and I was eleven. My sister heard of this. To separate us was just . . . unbelievable . . . no way. So she ran away from home, and they decided that this is another problem, so get rid of both of them. So we were sent then to a receiving home, then a group home. We were together. Just after I turned thirteen, my sister was the rambunctious one, outgoing. I was the quiet one, and they decided before *I* got into trouble, they would move me away, so they separated us. It didn't help because the place they moved me to wouldn't allow me to see my sister, because she's a problem child so we won't let her see her. So I ran away to be with her.

By then my brothers were old enough and on their own – the youngest one, twenty-two then, he was married and had a wife, and he decided to help out his little sisters. Then I was fourteen, she was thirteen. So he took her. Because I was doing okay where I was. I was still in a group home. I'd been in, how many group homes? I was in one, then another one, then I moved into, it was more of a foster home, and that in itself, that was another hard time. She accepted me as her daughter, but the rest of her family could not. Her sisters could not. I remember one Christmas, her sister came over, was taking presents out of a bag, and there was another girl who was staying there as a foster girl. They brought a present for her, and they didn't bring one for me. My foster mother's boyfriend said, I think you forgot something – he doesn't even live there, just over for the day, and he says, "You forgot somebody" – and she looks up at him with a straight face and says, "No I didn't. I've got all of the family." And I just . . . Everything in me just *went*. I couldn't . . . I got up, and I just walked upstairs real quiet. I didn't say a word. And I sat in my room. Later my foster mother came up and she apologized. But it just, I never forgot it, you know?

I was there til I was sixteen. My sister was living in another part of town. I ran away from the foster home, there was a real problem. I lived on the street for a while. My social worker, she says, "Well, okay, we can't have you living on the street, so we'll put you in a halfway house. The bill's paid there – if you're there, you're there." At this time I'm saying, I'm tired of all the places you're sticking me in. I'll be there, but I'll use it as a crash place, and she says, well as long as you report in there and you report to me that you're still alive and such. So I met this guy and I lived on the beach with him. Every morning we'd get up, go up to a friend's place and have a shower, some coffee, hang out til late at night, then go back down to the beach. So I spent a summer down there; that's when I met my husband. He was eight years older than me. I was seventeen, and he was twenty-five. This is not the guy from the beach. That guy left town – left me high and dry. This is another guy, we were together for a while. By this time I was almost seventeen and my worker was really starting to . . . you know, "You're going to have to start settling down. You're not going to school. You're not looking for jobs or anything." So my husband, before he was my husband, he said he would take care of me, and my worker agreed to it. I was allowed to live with him. I was still getting money; they paid my rent, supplied money for groceries, my clothes. It was as if I was living in a group home, but the money was going to me, with his consent. We were living in a house together, and one of the other people in the house decided they didn't like my boyfriend – they wanted him to leave but me to stay – so we had to move out. We were living in hotels. Between hotels for a while, on and off the streets.

After I turned eighteen I got pregnant. So my worker says, okay, enough of this running around. Are you keeping the baby or not? I says, Yes I'm keeping it, we're going to be married. She says, you

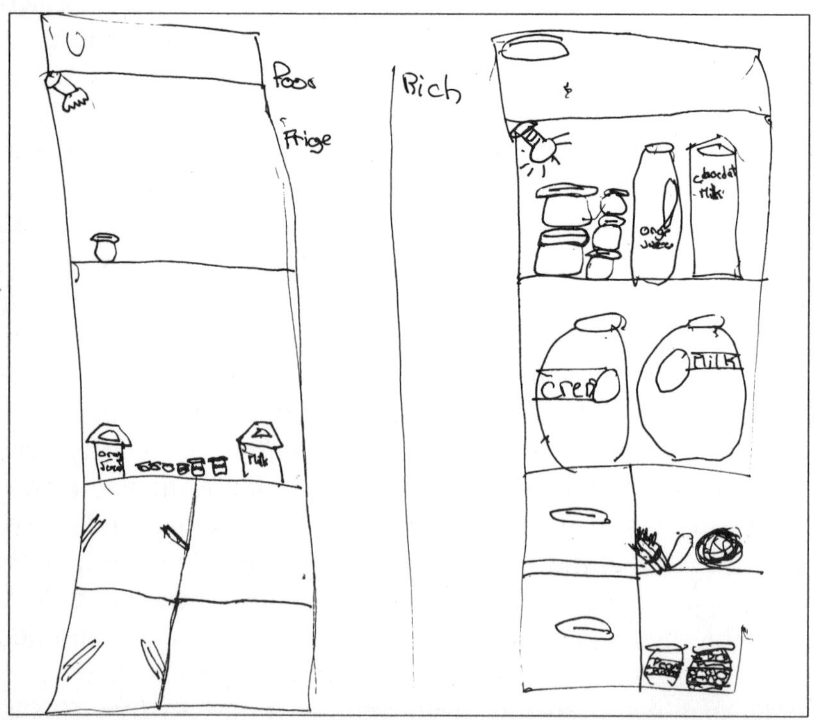

Daisy, age ten

can't marry. You're not of age yet. It just works out that a month after I turn nineteen, the baby's due. So I'll be of age, I can get married and have my baby. So we then found a decent hotel after all this running around. None of the places are even up anymore. They were torn down shortly after all of this.

Where did you get your street brothers and sisters from?

I wasn't a teenager on the street like most teenagers. I led a sheltered life in the group home. I never ran around on the street. I met my husband and, of course, nineteen years old, most kids are just finished all this running around. I was settling down to a family. It wasn't til I hit twenty-five that I started to be a person on the street. That's when I got all my street brothers and sisters, when I was twenty-five. I was a little bit older than them, but some were older than me. My dad now, he's from the street, he's older than me of course, in his mid-fifties. I can't even remember how I met him. Some people adopt me and some people I adopt that way. For him, he didn't get to see his kids; they're about my age. Just someone to talk to and then, after a while, because of his age, I said "Dad" one day, and he just looked at me like, "really?" You could see right away that he enjoyed the sound of it. After a bit, my children started calling him Grampa.

I would really love to get a job. I don't care if it pays enough to get off of welfare. But for my own pleasure. I was doing volunteer work, but I found some of the other volunteers – I didn't get along well with them, and I don't get paid for what I do as a volunteer.

If you had your choice, what would it be?

The real job of my choice? Working with children. I was volunteering at a school for a while, with kindergartens. I went to my worker at that time, this is a couple of years ago, and told her that the staff and the children at the school enjoyed me being there. The principal and other people wrote letters and I went in to my worker and told her, I've got a letter from this person, and I can get these letters. I want to do this. She turned to me and she says, That's a career. You shouldn't look for a career; you should look for a paying job.

When I was in a group home after my mom passed away, for years I'd wake up the rest of the kids in the group home,

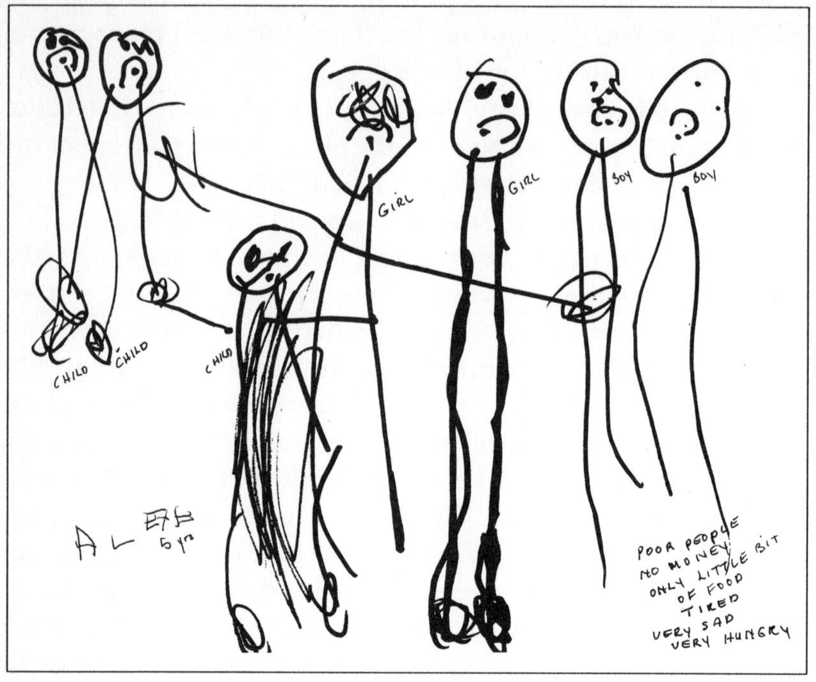

Poor people, no money, only little bit of food, tired, very sad, very hungry.

Alex, age five

screaming at my mother for leaving me and putting me here. That's after I was separated from my sister. I had nobody there, nobody to hold onto, nobody to hang onto, or anything. It only came out in my subconscious. I don't remember any of it. It was only from what I was told about what I did at night. I don't see my mom anymore in my sleep. Maybe it's good. I don't know. I have one picture left. My older brothers, they have pictures but they hang onto them. So I have a picture of my mom, she must be in her mid to late twenties. She was a young lady then. I look a lot like her. I am native, Irish, and Scottish, half Haida, quarter Cree, eighth Irish, and eighth Scottish. What a mixture, I know!

When I was younger, like I said, we were on welfare, but my mom always dressed us very, very nicely. I remember all the good dresses we had – gold sparkly one, blue checkered pattern one – I remember all of them. I had my oldest daughter, she was about two, I had her out one day and I'd just got her a jogging outfit. I saw this lady my mom took me to see when *I* was younger. She looks at my daughter and gets this smile on her face. She remembers how *my* mom dressed *me* umpteen years before, and now I've got a kid and I'm doing the same as she did. I think that reflects on my mom quite well. I'm proud of her.

I remember growing up – when you have kids and you're on welfare, not a lot of money, the thing my mom taught me, and I do with mine is, What do you really, really want? Cause you're not telling them, I can't afford what you want, all these other gifts. Just tell me what you really want and you're sure to get it. You give me a list of fifteen and I get you only five off of that, then you really don't get what you want. But if you give me only a list of what you really want, then you're letting them know you want to get them what they really want. And they learn from that. I've taught my two kids – they've learned when it comes round to Christmas time, they make a list – they have their wish list. It's twenty lists long – and then they have a Real List, and that may only have two or three things on it. That's what my mom taught me.

Barbara

Barbara is about twenty-six. Her story and her feelings were similar to mine in many ways. When she told me things, I would say, "Yeah, me too, me too. Yeah, I had coats on my bed as blankets. I didn't have much underwear either!"

❖

I was first aware that I was poor when I started to socialize, maybe six, seven. Having to borrow money from the neighbours, constantly. Never having a school bag, always carrying a plastic bag. Sometimes we'd be hungry; we would have bread that was fried in lard. Just the whole atmosphere of, you know . . . despair and poverty. My whole house stank of poverty and ignorance. It smells of pee, piss, just dirt. We used to have coats on the bed. You know, it was kinda like a fight. We had one fur coat and it used to get passed around. As well as that, the mattress had a big hook sticking up out of it. If you were lucky you wouldn't roll onto it, and three in the bed, sometimes four. The place always seemed to be in a mess from what I can remember. My mother was very depressed and she was always in bed. I'd be getting off to go to school, she was in bed. I wouldn't have lunch and I'd sometimes have to steal money from her to buy myself some lunch; I would end up buying sweets, candy and, you know, I always had this feeling of shame. I wasn't aware of hygiene; I hardly had clean underwear so it was really a shameful thing for me.

I used to try to . . . my survival instinct was, I developed a sense of humour. I used to try and put the shame onto other kids who I thought were worse than I was. My family always looked at other people and kind of looked at *their* poverty instead of looking at their own and had that weird twisted idea that we were better than other people in some ways. There were seven children; I was the third eldest.

School years were awful. I hated school. The first day I started school, my sister took me. I remember cursing my head off at the teacher. I was so horrified that the teacher wanted to take me. I didn't have . . . the basic security that a person needs in order to grow and branch out. I didn't have love . . . or closeness, just like the monkeys . . . when they're left on their own, they can't survive. Being lost and just so afraid of everything. You know, I'll never forget it. I was four years old. I cursed my head off at the teacher because I was so . . . I really needed to express that I didn't want to go with this woman.

How much school did you manage to get?

I left school when I was thirteen. By that time I had just developed an attitude. I was really known as the person they would throw outside the door, you know? I was always joking around and just doing things that were just for a laugh to give everybody a laugh. They didn't like me for that. They just wanted to pass me through. There was just one teacher that I remember that was okay with me. I used to write stories and she would let me read them to the class. I really liked her and she showed me that extra attention, but that was about the only thing I ever liked about school.

I left school and got a job in a sewing factory, at thirteen. I lied and said I was older. Things didn't get better from there. I didn't have any skills. I didn't have any people skills. I didn't have any kind of life skills. I was just thrown into the deep end with it, and I was just abused. The abuse continued, just like . . . Situations I was in, it was just a whirlpool of abuse, you know. At that time I was actually glad to be working so that I had some money to buy my own clothes and really feel like I was my own person because from the time I was born, my clothes were hand-me-downs so I pretended that I was fifteen or sixteen. I stayed at home until I moved to Canada. I gave my mother my pay packet and she gave me back a small amount. But I felt good. I was earning money. It was really hard.

How has that affected your expectations of life?

I don't know. I always had this feeling, this feeling of fear. I grew up with this feeling. It was a feeling that I woke up with in the morning. This feeling of not knowing what I was about, where I was going, what disaster was going to happen to me. I went through it for years until . . . I consider myself to have been illiterate until the age of twenty-one, and I kind of got by. And my writing was like a child of, I don't think you would even say a thirteen-year-old, because they are probably more literate than I was at the time. I didn't do homework, I never worked in school. I always had a desire to learn, but I never knew how. I would try to read and I would try to concentrate. I never had a concentration span. I just always thought I was backward. I never had

A family with no money is not rich. They don't have a penny or a dime. They are poor. They feel sad.

Kim, age eight

encouragement or anything like that, so I didn't really know that it was important and that it would be a tool in helping me to know myself and to sort of see the world in a clearer picture. I think, when you grow up in poverty, that's the least of people's worries. It's something that goes on through the generations in my family. My mother left school when she was very young and . . . she had seven children with just my father working and she needed money, you know.

When I came to Canada, I met this guy and he was going to university and he was studying English and philosophy. That was nothing to me. I wasn't impressed at all because I couldn't appreciate it. He encouraged me to go back to school and to upgrade. I have Grade 12 now.

I have a clearer picture on life and I'm more confident about who I am. This is a process that has been going on for the past few years, of doing some inner work, of looking at my past and how it has affected me up to now.

Is there anything you want to say about childhood poverty?

Myself, I feel that some people can get out of it. I feel that I've been blessed and that's why I can look at it objectively now. I'm still in a poor situation, but at least I have tools to get out of it, to help myself. There are some people who don't have that opportunity. I don't think we have enough tools out there. There are literacy programs, but they are just marginal programs. They need to be more aware of poverty in schools. If they were more aware of it in the schools, they could be more sensitive to the children, have some kind of discussions. When I was in school, I needed love, that's what I needed. I needed someone to understand, to tell me what was going on. I didn't know, 'cause when you're right in there, when you're right in poverty, you don't know. Especially if you're a child. How do you know? You don't know anything else.

For me, I think the future looks brighter for me . . .

Laura

Laura is a young woman, in her early twenties. She wrote about her childhood for me.

❖

From my childhood I carry the fear, guilt, and shame of poverty. Underneath the anger, resentment, and rigid control, I was searching for security and continue to. It takes constant determination, even as an adult with a very secure job and loving friends and family, not to lose control, lash out, or become needy and forlorn. All from the fear, the life-threatening fear, of a helpless child without adequate food, a safe environment from violence and drugs and abuse, a sense of routine and knowing, enough emotional support and attention, without a sense of self or self worth.

At five, my mother and father separated. Although this relieved much of the abuse, it took my brother from me and left my mother and I with $32. Young children cut off to survive. They do not consciously feel their defensive struggle or the shame of being different. But they know they are not as good as others. I remember the thrill of finding chocolate in a Safeway garbage during our nightly raids. I know my mom couldn't say no since it was free.

It was my experience of public education, as well as mass media's influence, that made it all too apparent that there was something wrong with me. I didn't have a nice house, the right toys, a TV, a dad. I couldn't hang out with the kids who went to McDonald's for lunch and bowling or to the movies. I would lie and sometimes steal, using friends so I could play with their toys, eat their food, and imagine their parents were mine.

When I was very young, we couldn't afford daycare so I had to take the bus to my mother's work after school. Restless and bored, I resented my mother for this. I wanted to go to the park, have a snack and watch cartoons, go home and play with the latest toy, while my mother made me a snack and my father came home from work and gave me a hug. But I knew I was different, and I couldn't let it show. I was abused and molested in the neighbourhood where we lived several times. Although child abuse is not particular to children below the poverty line, in nearly every case I would not have suffered if we had adequate money. For example, if I didn't do laundry alone at night at the age of eight; if I had had a babysitter to take me to the park; if there weren't drug dealers living in our basement; if I hadn't lied to my friend's parents about where I lived – I walked right into a stranger's house, pretending to live there, until my ride had left and I was "safe" to walk home in the dark alone.

My mother had to work constantly and creatively to get food, clothes, and shelter. She was physically and emotionally exhausted, she had a headache, or couldn't walk because of her back. Once my father abandoned my delinquent teenage brother, she became unable to cope with the mess, the fighting, stealing, lying. The bitter pressure from my brother and I blaming her for all we could not have. The strength, ingenuity, and political insight of my mother, I now know is what has given me the chance to break the poverty cycle. She explained our context and encouraged me to be realistic in her responses to my pressure. "Would you rather live in a nice house or eat?" But I did not understand economics then. I felt I was being punished, eating porridge day in and out, looking like a fool in my Sally Ann clothes and mismatched socks. I was humiliated when the paper read "Little Laura has a leaky roof" after my mother's encouragement to write a letter if I was angry about moldy water dripping on my bed when I was trying to sleep. I was seen on TV by my friends, receiving an Xmas charity dinner. I was exposed and ridiculed, and angry at my mother's excitement for us to have a good meal. Much of my mother's skills and determination which enabled us to break the cycle, came from her middle-class background. Her strength and dignity came from the ability to understand our situation in its societal context. She helped me make the political connections and to learn that my environment is not a reflection of my self worth but a reflection of a social and political system which denies equal opportunity and value of human life.

This poem is in admiration of my mother and all single mothers whose children are pressuring, blaming, lying, stealing,

A family has no milk, no home, no bed, and they feel mad and sad, and they don't have no cups or plates, no clothes.

Mel, age eight

doing drugs, and fighting to find a sense of acceptance and worth under the poverty line.

My picture of her is no longer mad
She could not give me more than she had
The love she gave has grown in time
I could not choose a mother as fine
Always there, giving hers for me
to find mine, kind and strong
but exhausted from the game
sucked dry from shame
She kept herself intact calling on
her own love, living on her own right,
giving up the fight,
sacrificing on the outside day after day
waiting for a way out.
Saving, scrimping, and stretching out her hands to feed me.
Holding me back from the bitter stabs of reality,
getting me ready to fight for myself.
But never to leave me, always open with her care.
She had to let me go not knowing how I'd fare.

She stayed waiting for my return for myself to share.
Eager to know, clear about what's fair
sometimes overtired, but I know the love is there,
was there, stays there and grows.
Every little light, birthday surprises and late nights,
skating lessons and worry fights,
handmade dresses and dolls that dance
any time there was a chance
for me to fly
you let me try.
You let me be me and try it all,
still standing by to catch me when I fall.
It is but for your love that I am standing tall.

Eve

I was talking with Eve about interviewing her son. We started to talk about her life. We were talking on the phone. This is what she told me.

❖

I was an army child in Winnipeg. I had no confidence as far back as I could remember. My family worked. There were five kids. I was the second eldest. From age nine to twelve all I did was housework and taking care of the children, bathing them, cooking for them, scrubbing floors. I always felt that I could do nothing right. I left school in Grade 9. I was sixteen. I hitchhiked to Vancouver with a guy, but we split up. It was easier to get a ride that way. All I had was the clothes I was wearing. I slept out in Stanley Park under the trees, by myself. I would go into the city and panhandle. My weight was 160 when I left Winnipeg. I went down to 110 in one month.

When I was sleeping out in Stanley Park, it was late August, early September. It was warm in the day, but cold at night. The ground was damp. When I arrived in the city, I sat on the sidewalk and cried. I had no home, no clothes. I couldn't wash my hair or bathe. I used gas station washrooms. Boy, did I ever smell.

I would stay hidden and avoid people, just bum money downtown then sleep in the park. One night the cops found me. I said, "I've nowhere to go, I'm not bothering anybody, let me stay." They searched my purse and found rolling papers and accused me of having drugs. Anyway, they let me stay but told me I had to be out of the park at sunrise. I had nowhere to go. I didn't know about hostels and that kind of stuff.

After three weeks I stayed at the YWCA for a couple of days in a dorm. They gave me meal tickets. I didn't like it there. I didn't like the other women there, so I went back to the park for a few days.

I had a penpal in Vancouver so I looked him up and told him a big story that my mother was sick and dying and that I needed to get back home, so he gave me a bus ticket to Winnipeg. I didn't go home. I squatted in abandoned houses. They were cold. It was winter and the hydro had been turned off. I was scared of getting raped, but it didn't happen. I panhandled to live . . .

I went home when I was nearly seventeen. My parents were glad that I was alive. But they were not that welcoming. They said, if you want to stay, get a job and pay room and board. I got a job in a laundry for really low pay. You know, where they put the towels in the big rollers. Me and a friend took off for an afternoon, so we got fired. My mother was pissed off. She said, I want you and your stuff out of here before I get home. I was really hurt. I had no money. I hitchhiked to Vancouver. I lived in a hippy crash pad. I got a place with three other girls. I got a job in a doughnut store. It was really for peanuts. It didn't work out. I couldn't pay my share of the rent, so they kept all my stuff. They said they were keeping my stuff until I paid my share of the rent. I said, piss on them.

I was still a virgin. I went to Commercial and decided to prostitute. I picked up a big fat Italian. I did it for ten dollars. Honest. I was a virgin. I took the ten dollars, had a shower, felt really gross. Gave them the ten dollars and said give me ten dollars worth of my stuff. I took some jeans and underwear, not much.

I went back to the hippy crash pad. It was called Cool Aid. It was a house near Seventh and Burrard. Cool Aid it was called, you know, like the drink. It was painted in psychedelic colours – hot pinks, greens, orange – really bright . . . a bunch of hippies lived there. Everyone was stoned, so stoned that it didn't matter who stayed there. I was free to hang out and maybe contribute two dollars. I did pot and LSD. I liked it. I hitchhiked downtown to get some LSD. I met a guy at Fourth and Burrard. He said, I got some LSD. I said, Okay. I moved in with him. I got pregnant, got married, neither of us knew what love was all about. When my daughter was three years old, I caught him fooling around. We were living on an island. I left him and came back to Vancouver. I had odd jobs and welfare. I got into cocaine. The people who I knew, the people I hang out with, were doing it. They offered. I said sure, why not?

I was shooting up. The guy I was getting it from said, I trust you; pay me later. I would do under-the-table jobs to try and pay him. Finally, after a year, I owed him $900. It was taking everything I had to pay him. So I decided to get out. I threw the needles away and went to Pemberton to dry out, although I still drank beer and smoked pot. While I was there, my second husband left. He was nuts. He tried to kill me. He was really nuts. My daughter was about six years old. This older man, a grampa type, was babysitting my daughter from when she was six til she was eleven. I thought maybe my husband had molested her, but she said no. This old guy had been molesting her all along and I never knew it. When George was born, I let him babysit him for three years. I trusted the guy. It turned out he was molesting George too.

How I found out was, when my daughter was seventeen and living in Vancouver, she was going for counselling, so she came and told me about that old man, what he had done, and that she thought he was abusing George too. She said he had stopped abusing her when she was eleven because she had told him she didn't want to do it anymore. I trusted that guy for eleven years. If I had had a gun, I would have blown him away. I got a gun. I was going to shoot him. I said, watch me. I'm gonna shoot him. I hated myself for not knowing. I hated myself. The kids used to have sleepovers at his house. I trusted him. My child's father said, let me go and talk to him. He came back and said he admitted abusing Chrissy but not George.

The police and social workers got involved, but George was only three and he couldn't talk. They used dolls, tapes, but he wouldn't talk. Chrissy decided not to go to court. She said she just wanted to get on with her life. George goes to a psychiatrist and a social worker. He is eight. He likes his psychiatrist and his worker.

So nothing has been done. That old man is still up in Pemberton. All the police could do, because there was no legal evidence, was to tell him he is not allowed to babysit. He is still there. Nothing happened to him.

Mary

Mary is a young woman about twenty-five years of age. She has been an active volunteer at a community centre that I go to. She had approached me and said, "I would like to be in your book. There are some things I would like to say."

This picture mean when I was poor it was hard for me to live with my mom when she didn't work. We didn't had any food. My birthday wasn't celebrated. I cryed a lot that my mom started forgetting where she put her things. I didn't stayed home. I stayed with my uncle. My aunt stayed with my mom all the time until she got better. It was so hard. My uncle was there for us. He give my mom money to get her live going.

Joe, age eleven

❖

When I was little, we lived on welfare. My mom, she couldn't work.

Kindergarten was okay. It wasn't til I got to Grade 1 and, this story I relate to people all the time. We had a teacher who . . . what an idiot, stupid teacher. I'm left-handed; she gave me right-handed scissors, then wanted to put me in a slow class because I couldn't use them. That was one incident. I was always, like, certain classes I took were special classes, but what they failed to realize was, I was having so many problems at home, it wasn't that I couldn't learn because I had learning disabilities, it was just so much stress at home.

I first realized I was poor at maybe four or five. I felt embarrassed and ashamed at school because even things like having a "family doctor," I didn't have one when I was little. It was really embarrassing. They'd go, "Who's your family doctor?" And I'd say, "I don't have one," and people would say, "You don't have a family doctor?!"

Poverty was always having to ask for handouts, things like "What does your dad do for a living?" "Nothing." When I was ten he got a job as a cab driver.

Home there was physical abuse, lots of abuse, sexual abuse . . . all kinds of things. My mom was being beaten up by my dad. He was a real bastard.

Did you ever tell anybody in school?

I had a chance to tell a social worker, but I said no. Someone reported all the stuff, and I said no . . .

Why?

I don't know. I was terrified of him. My dad always said I was stupid and I know by the way they treated me in school they thought I was stupid. Never paid me any attention. Never bothered to ask me if I needed help. They just tossed me aside like I was yesterday's newspaper.

In Grade 10 I had a good teacher. I had him one year and I didn't try. I came back the next year and he said, are you going to try in my class, because if you're not going to try, get the hell out of my class. So I tried in his class, and I got a good grade in his class because I tried. He kept encouraging me to try. He told me that trying was more important than succeeding. He said, if you fail trying, that's more important than not trying at all. He was a really nice person.

I graduated with not enough credits – I needed twelve and I had eight. I got my GED [General Equivalency Diploma] a couple of years ago. I tried to run away from home, but I ended up always going back the next day. One time I ran away, my dad beat me up and I ran away and I went to the Lux Theatre just down on Hastings. I stayed there and watched movies, and then I want home, but I didn't want to go in so I went under the picnic table. I was gone all night. Often I would just go to my friend's house for the night.

How did the abuse stop?

My dad left my mother.

Why has he never been charged with sexual abuse?

No point . . . I just want him to leave me alone.

Did he abuse your other family members?

We don't talk about it.

How are you dealing with it?

Counselling, stuff like that.

Do you still see your dad?

Hell, no way . . . no way.

What does having no money mean?
No food in the cart.

Lisa, age six

How do you feel when you do see him?

Hurt now, but before, angry . . . oh, angry, angry!

What if he's abusing other children?

I don't know. That's not my responsibility.

After my dad left, I stayed home, took care of my mom. I drank, took drugs. Eventually I became a nervous wreck. My mom died. She had a brain hemorrhage. That was very difficult. I don't know if I loved her. I was so emotionally attached to her. In between my dad leaving my mom and my mom dying, I met my husband. I lived with my sister for a year after my mother died. That wasn't working out; we were just killing each other. And then I lived with him for a year. I had just forgotten or repressed all the things that had happened to me. Then as I lived with him, the more I felt safer, it all started coming out and then all of a sudden, bang. It was like POW! I cracked up, I cracked up. I couldn't work anymore. I ended up quitting my job that I had. I actually even collected welfare a couple of times. Then I got a job where I met my husband. But I quit that one. I got stressed out and I quit, and then I got another job, and that job I quit because I couldn't function anymore, and then I had to go in for counselling for three years. Like, on and off I'd work in between, when I wasn't in counselling, and I just was a wreck, couldn't think straight, couldn't function . . . I went off drugs a long time ago, when I was twenty.

How are things now?

Good . . . Being a wife, my goals are to be a good mother, not the kind of mother I had, that didn't care. I think my husband would make a good father.

Most of the jobs I've found are minimum wage jobs, no medical, no dental, work hard and get no money. I lived with other people. I was lucky that way; if I had had to live on my own, I would have ended up living in a hotel room. I wouldn't have been able to live.

What do you think being
poor means?
*A Christmas tree
with only two decorations –
the light has no shade
on it – 3 children and
only 1 present.*
Lana, age six

Kathryn

Kathryn wrote this for It's Time Women Speak Out, *a report produced by Housewives in Training and Research in 1987. I included it in my first book,* No Way to Live.

Recently, I listened to a teacher read some excerpts from children's class journals at a public forum on hunger in Vancouver schools. These children wrote statements about their hunger and shame, and one child wrote of waiting for the next welfare cheque when the money ran out.

Listening brought back old feelings. I remember very clearly how it felt to be hungry as a child. The empty ache was so overwhelming that I had to fight to hold back the tears. We weren't always hungry, but I will never forget the times we were. I used to sit in my class unable to concentrate on anything but the knowledge that I would have to watch the other children eating at recess and lunch time. I remember that I isolated myself from the other children and watched them, imagining that someone would share their food with me.

When there was enough money for something extra, we had fruit. My mother always gave it to my brother and I. Now, years later, if my mother is offered fruit, she refuses it. When she was young, she loved to eat fruit, but she spent so many years refusing it that she developed an aversion to it. I know that, given similar circumstances, I would do the same thing, nevertheless I feel guilty, because I think it would be better for her health if she would eat fruit.

I wasn't crying by myself in that forum. Other women, possibly women who didn't have enough money to last the month to feed their children, were exposing more of their frustration and anguish than I was.

I am uncomfortable with the term "child poverty" because it isolates children from their mothers. When children are hungry, it is because their mothers are hungry. If I had one piece of bread in the house it would be for my child, not for myself. This is true for all mothers.

Sheila

That damn period had come again. She, ten years old, worried where she could find the money for sanitary pads. The old people she was staying with in the country were angry. Her parents were way behind with payments for her keep. The old lady would say, your parents don't care about you. What kind of parents don't send money for their kids? No money came for her allowance either. Her clothes were worn. One kind lady altered a dress of her own and gave it to her. It was quite pretty.

Worried and scared because her period had come, she knocked on a farmer's door. The farmer's wife knew her because she played with her children. She quietly asked the farmer's wife for a sanitary pad. The farmer's wife gave her a homemade one, a square piece of cloth that folded up into a rectangle and had stitched holes in it. Complicated, but she did manage to figure it out.

❖

It was during my most battered time that I took a class in domestic science at school. I think I was about nine. I'm not sure.

This teacher was young and smiled and made cooking fun, and when I didn't have the money to pay for what we had cooked, she would quietly let me go without paying. She liked me.

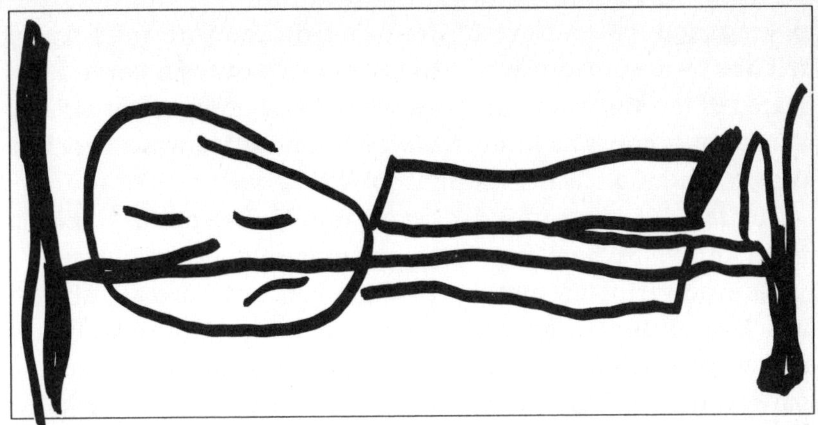

What do you think being poor means?
Going to bed hungry.

Kelly, age seven

She told the class that her father was retired and that if any of us had any questions we wanted answered, we could give them to her and she would bring the answers the following week.

It was wonderful. I wanted to know why the earth moved, how it moved, where did the sun come from . . . She answered all my questions.

By her gestures and her tone of voice and her smile, I knew she liked me. One day it was freezing cold. She looked down at my sockless feet with the tennis shoes that had holes so big my toes hung out. She said, "Aren't your feet cold, dear?" I lied and said, "Oh no, I like them this way." Strange, I always lied to cover up my abuse and neglect. She was a wonderful teacher. Very wise.

❖

She was very thin, with short dark hair, a short sharp nose. She looked a little like the Wicked Witch of the West in the Wizard of Oz. She was the English teacher, a nervous, high-strung woman with an unpleasant high-pitched voice. She seemed like a very angry person.

One day during lunch hour there was a violent thunderstorm. The room turned dark. She was on lunch duty. I was about eleven. I was scared, so I touched her arm, quite gently. I guess I wanted some reassurance that everything was going to be safe.

She screamed. "Don't touch me . . . Don't touch me . . . Never

never touch me . . . Never!" Her face twitched with total rage. I felt like I was someone who had just crawled out of a sewer. I was scared of the storm, but more scared of her. Because I was already abused at home, this just confirmed for me that I was a very bad person, and if a teacher thought so, then I must be.

Her face is forever imposed on my mind, like a photo you keep in an album. Strange, but that is my only memory of her.

How powerful teachers are. How many of us were really abused in school. I think if the stories could be told, we would perhaps realize that schools created much more dysfunction than the parents did, yet the blame was always on the parents, totally, instead of really looking at the whole picture.

One of my very best friends is a teacher. Her name is Marlene. She teaches at Deep Cove. I went with her to see her class, helped her wash off some books at the end of the year. She is warm, loving, caring, and really does love her students. She wears washable clothes so that kids can touch her. I wish she could have been my teacher.

❖

Sheila's Battle with Mr. Smith

The eleven year old with budding breasts
opened the door
of Mr. Smith's beer store
darkly lit with wooden beamed ceilings,
creaky dirty wooden floor
and of course, at the counter
the pale faced, beady eyed Mr. Smith
who always stared at her breasts
Mr. Smith's father had hung himself
from those beams
years ago it was said
she was scared
of Mr. Smith
and the ghost of his father
Some nights she had to go to the store
more than once
it depended on how drunk

her mother was
Anxiously she would watch
the large screw-top beer bottles become empty
knowing that she would have to return
to Mr. Smith's beer store
to beady eyed Mr. Smith
If the store was empty
he would come around the counter
and try to fondle
her breasts
usually she managed to wriggle away
Mr. Smith was at the counter that special day
Mr. Smith said, come round here
come behind the counter
she said, no no I don't want to
Mr. Smith said, but you are just like your mother
you are your mother's daughter
Come here, come behind the counter
I want to show you something
She became enraged
fear left her
she yelled and pounded her small fists
    on the counter
I'll never drink
I won't smoke
I'll never hurt my children
and she never did
and Mr. beady eyed pale faced Smith
never bothered her again
and she was no longer scared
he was just a dirty old man
who owned a beer store
No woman or child should ever accept labels
    from beady eyed smiths

❖

She, fifteen years of age, was working as a kennel maid plus house maid. The dogs were huge St. Bernards. She worked hard. She walked the dogs two at a time. There were ten dogs. She fed them and groomed them, cleaned up their messes. She washed the dishes, many of them, because there were boarders in the house. When the daughter of the owners went dancing, she helped her dress and powdered her back for her. She fantasized that she was a real-life Cinderella, but there was no fairy godmother.

One dog was vicious. He was kept for breeding. She didn't have to take care of him. He would growl and snarl when anyone passed his cage.

She hated the shed. Huge chunks of raw horse meat hung from the roof in clumps (food for the dogs). When she went in to get the feed, the meat terrified her as it brushed against her hair. Mr. Grimes, the owner, looked at her in a real weird way that made her feel very uncomfortable. She always made sure that she wasn't alone in the shed with him. She was allowed one afternoon off a week, that would be after she had scrubbed all the floors, on her hands and knees of course.

Mr. Grimes said, "Come with me into the shed. I want to show you something."

She went nervously. He showed her a bench with straps on it. He said, "Tomorrow we are going to mate Jessica with Rex." Rex was the vicious dog, and remember, these were huge St. Bernard dogs. "We will have to strap Jessica to this bench," he explained,

A mum and child, only 3 things in the fridge. No supper.

Stevy, age eight

"and you will have to help me. We will do it early tomorrow morning."

She went back into the house. All her instincts said, run, run, you're in danger. She went up to the room at the top of the third flight of stairs, threw her clothes into her bag as swiftly as she could, quietly, so quietly, walked down the stairs out of the front door, down the street, walking swiftly and determinedly into freedom. The street was safer, much safer, than what she had left behind.

It was my final year of school in the English education system. I had been to so many schools over the years that it's hard to even count them. I had stayed with a family, a relative, for the last year of school, in return for chores and the money that my father often didn't send. My father had started a second-hand clothing store, so I had a few nice dresses. We had a male teacher, a tall man, about thirty-five, dark hair, glasses. He constantly told me how bright I was, and that I could do very well. I remember him praising me, showing me that he liked me. He smiled and said to me, "Sheila, you can do anything you want. You have the capabilities and a good brain." At the end of the year I graduated with good marks. I was ready for the workforce. I was fifteen. I went to search for my teacher. I think I may have had a crush on him. After all, he had shown me such kindness. Anyway, I wanted to kiss him goodbye, but he was a very wise man and just smiled at me, shook my hand, and wished me good luck. I can still remember how special he made me feel.

A child bride. The night before the wedding she, just seventeen, sewed up the huge hole in the crotch of his only pair of non-working pants, pressed them, washed and ironed his shirt to get ready for their wedding day. She had paid a couple of dollars for a second-hand white dress with polka dots and red roses that she thought was really nice, because it came just below her knees and she could wear it after the event. She had known the man she was to marry about five months. The truth was, she would have married anyone just to have a home. They had rented a furnished room that had a hot plate and a nice window and a shared bathroom down the hall. That was going to be her home after the wedding.

Her grandmother had said, why are you getting married? You ain't knocked up and you are the same as when you were born. She didn't like him, the husband-to-be.

Come the great day, she left from her grandmother's house, walked down the street around the corner, got on a bus, and went to the registry office with her grandmother. Her father showed up, really relieved to be getting rid of any responsibility towards her, not that he had ever shown much.

A few words were said which she didn't hear, a ring that they had bought at a pawn shop for a few dollars was put on her finger. She was now married. Her father splurged and took everyone for a cup of tea (no cakes) to a close-by, cheap café. An hour later her new husband said, "You're my wife now. Let's go home and you can cook my supper." The child bride dutifully went home and peeled potatoes, cooked and mashed them, and fried the greasy sausages.

People Who Work With Children

Peggie

Peggie is a worker in the Family Advancement Program at an east side school.

❖

What kind of problems have you had getting services for children?

We've had lots of trouble getting our kids into counselling. Last year we had lots of children disclosing sexual abuse and the usual waiting list was six months to twelve months before they would get in for an assessment or for any type of counselling, so in the meantime, they went without any service.

What about the investigation?

That part was even more frustrating. We encourage our kids to make reports, which they do, and they talk to the police and the social workers, but after the interview is done, there were several incidents where the kids didn't even hear from a police person for five or six months. There's just too many cases for the, I think it's twelve workers they have down there. It could be a year before the alleged abuser is even interviewed.

If children had money for counselling, could they get counselling?

There are lots of private practitioners that are available. They also have a waiting list, but it's certainly not six months to a year. But they do charge. An hourly rate is sixty to a hundred dollars an hour. Our parents can not afford to pay that. It's a scary thing. They finally make a disclosure, the police will come out and interview them, and for lots of kids that's the last they see or hear of their case for months. I'm talking ten to twelve months.

There's a big frustration with the police department. I think they need to get more police officers that are, first of all, aware of how to work with kids that have been abused, are sensitive to that. As well, there needs to be more funding for more of them on the police department.

Another issue is, it's not the parent's fault. A lot of times the parents don't have a wide support network or family network, therefore, in order to have a break for them to get out and do what they need to do, they rely on neighbours, they rely on anybody that's going to take care of their kids. And those people don't always turn out to be the best people to take care of their children. Then again, it's not their problem, it's society's problem that there isn't adequate childcare services available to them.

Which brings me to an example of a child who was abused by somebody in the community and this person is still in the community. Since then, this person has abused about four other children, and the police are not responding quickly enough as far as I'm concerned.

How long a time lag from the first complaint?

Over one year. It was the beginning of last school year. They're not working on that very quickly. They're just too busy.

What happens when a child divulges sexual abuse?

Well, they'll take the report and usually interview and videotape the child, but it's afterwards where there's a lack of service. There's no follow-through for the kids. The kids feel like, "Wow, I've told this big secret, but now what's going to happen?" The abuser's still in the community. They still see the child. The child is not safe.

One child made a report. Social Services interviewed. They didn't feel there was enough for them to go on, so the child was still left in an environment which was unsafe. The abuse continued. The second time he did disclose, they listened to him. The man was removed from the home, but he's still in the community. He sees him on the bus; he sees him at McDonald's, and he's afraid. He has not been prosecuted. He hasn't even been interviewed.

Why?

They are busy down there. They can't get hold of him. They make appointments for him to come in to make a statement; he doesn't show up.

How serious is this charge in your opinion?

I think it's very serious. It's sexual abuse that involved all aspects of sex with a ten-year-old. I'm not talking about just fondling. I'm talking about . . . it went much farther . . . and I find it very alarming that he's still out there, and I phone the constables and I say, I'm really worried, not only for the community but I'm worried for the child. They say sorry, we have people calling like you every single day. We can not respond to them quicker. We get ten files put on our desk every morning.

Are the children checked for AIDS and STD? The abuser could have infected them.

Children are usually medicaled at Children's Hospital. A whole medical test is done on them, and I believe AIDS is one of the tests they do.

So the reality is, a ten-year-old has been raped. He has to go through all that testing . . . ?

And is still feeling guilty for telling. He feels like he wasn't believed. His relationship with his mother is very negative now. He is very angry with mom for letting this happen. Mom has gotten to the point that she's feeling she might have to put him in care. She's got no resources, no family to help her out. Treatment for him . . . it's been a year since we first referred him, and now he's finally getting sexual abuse counselling. The man hasn't been charged.

Why?

This is my question. I have been told because he won't come in and testify.

If this were a child from an affluent community whose family had money, would it be different?

I'm not saying that their lawyer is not very good. I think the lawyer they had – from Legal Aid – is probably a very good lawyer, an adequate lawyer, but also he has too many cases to deal with. If they had money, they would probably get a lawyer with a private practice. Push it along. And maybe a mother who felt she had a bit more power in this would be calling every day, maybe writing letters to the appropriate people, and getting it going. It would probably be very different. Poverty affects these kids in every aspect. Forty to fifty percent of the kids here live below the poverty line. It affects them in how they're parented; it affects how they feel about themselves in the school, how other kids treat them. It affects even the way some teachers see them, because it's a preconceived idea – they're poor, maybe their parents are drinkers, maybe their brother's an alcoholic. I can't say all teachers are like that, but I've definitely been in rooms where kids are talked about that way. You know – "That kid comes from this family" . . . "They must drink all their money away." Even though there is no proof. So kids therefore are labelled at the beginning and I think they're only going to advance as far as that label allows them. They're not going to advance to their full potential that way.

We had a twelve-year-old girl a few years ago, who came from a home where there was an incredible amount of problems. Her parents were dealing with their own issues, and this child ended up being sexually abused because she wanted some attention and there was a man in the community that gave her some attention. He abused her for over a year. The abuse involved sex. She started doing very badly in school, her grades dropped, she was aggressive and angry at everybody – she had a lot of bitterness. School became such a negative place for her to be, she decided not to come to school. She told a friend finally about the abuse and Social Services became involved, and there is an investigation with the police and, again, it's been another one of those year investigations. The guy is still in the community. He hasn't been prosecuted. I understand there is a court case set for next year. By the time it gets to court, it will be almost two years. In all that time, he's in the community. I would be very scared, as a parent.

Anyway, this child started not coming to school because it was too negative. She was called names. She felt very bad about herself. Then it got to the point that she didn't want to be at home either, that was too much of an unpleasant environment for her. So she just left and started sleeping at friend's houses, and when she wore out her welcome was basically on the streets, twelve years old. We were able, after five or six weeks of her being on the streets, to get her to agree that she should live in a foster home. But the problem with that is, sure, she's finally agreed to that; it's been five months we've been looking for a foster home and we can't come up with one for her so she's in a group home in the meantime. She finally started sexual abuse counselling, so that almost took a year as well.

You must be so frustrated. How are you feeling?

If you had asked me this last June when I finished, I would have told you that I was incredibly frustrated with the system. It takes more out of me than the actual work with the kids. I feel a little refreshed after the summer, and I have energy to give to the kids. The program that I work for, Family Advancement, is the only program that's in the schools for the kids, for the families. We don't work for the school board, so there's total confidentiality. It's preventative. I have parents that write me letters and

If you're being sexually abused then it is okay for you to say No. Don't be afraid. Lots of people will believe you. If you don't tell someone then they could be sexually abusing someone else. Maybe even best friend or a sister or brother. You're not a dummy. Be aware that people like that are out there and they look like an everyday person you meet. When you say no you will feel lots better and believe me. I do know how it feels. So it is okay to say No.

Patty, age eleven

say, "What would we do without you? You were the only person there for us, that helped us through the whole process." I do counselling with kids, I do play therapy, art therapy with them. I am the only person that can see them right away, right when the crisis is. I don't have to put them on a waiting list. I don't have to do an income test, none of that.

This is a big jar of worms, the lid is off, and there does not seem to be the resources to deal with it. Children are being forced to live on the street?

I think it has a lot to do with people now coming out in the open about their abuses. For so long it was just not talked about. People are coming out in the open, they want to get help, they don't want these cycles to repeat with their families. The resources aren't out there – unless you've got money or are willing to wait on their waiting list. There are certainly a lot of practitioners who will take you on. Victim's Compensation often will pay for these services, but that's another process; you fill in an application, you wait three, four, five months for them to reply. In the meantime nothing is happening for the kids.

We've had cases of young boys abusing other young boys in the community. One wonders where they've learnt this behaviour. Stats show that most kids who abuse have been abused themselves. It's much more difficult because boys don't talk as much. They're interviewed and I've seen some for counselling, but they will not talk about it, therefore they don't deal with it and their way is to reenact it. So in our school we're faced with the problem of, how do we keep our kids safe? We have to start placing rules for certain kids who can't stay for lunch, they can't stay for recess, and then they become labelled as "different."

I feel in order for there to be any changes, it has to start with the family. With single-parent families, there has to be more opportunities for them to get back into the workforce. There's got to be more support once they are there. Wages have to be higher. They can not survive on minimum wage with their kids. They're trying their best, but they just can't. Their kids don't get to go out on the weekends, and they start to feel guilty. Parents need to be empowered. There needs to be some work in the schools. Teachers need to be made aware of what kind of kids are coming to our school. They need to be made aware that poverty is a problem, that kids are no different because they are poor. They need to be sensitive to that and not treat kids any differently. Therefore, we need to have more education, we need to do more programs for teachers to be aware of that.

I think there needs to be more money placed in treatment programs. The police need to have more sexual abuse squad members to deal with the problems. We need to work as a whole. I think everybody's doing their little bit everywhere, but there's no real network. Nobody is working together. We are not going to get very far. There has to be some kind of approach where everyone deals with this problem together, everyone is aware of it. Pieces start to fit then. I think we all have some power, but I'm talking about the real power, people who are making our laws, making our budgets. I want them to realize and recognize the extent of the problem we have here with kids and parents and families living in poverty, and how it affects the kids, and to look at our kids as our future, and if our kids are not getting their needs met now, what kind of citizens are we going to have? Because the kids are not getting their needs met now. They're going to be in jail, they're going to be hooking by the time they're twelve, they're going to be doing drugs. The reason they're not getting their needs met is, there's not enough programs, there's not enough money, there's not enough funding. The priority is not where it needs to be. The funding has to change. We need to priorize our children and their needs, and this can be done through funding for more treatment and support services. Can we as a society blame these children if they turn to the street or drugs or crime when their needs have not been met by us?

Immigrant and refugee children often live on less than regular welfare, no medical, no family allowance while their status is being determined. No extras for kids, no funds for camp or after-school programs. They have often suffered losses, torture, culture shock. Schools may not be as friendly and welcoming to other cultures. The climate is colder. Parents have told me they feel looked down upon.

Battered women and their families often stay in abusive situations because either they don't feel comfortable in a shelter, or there's no vacancy in a shelter. When children are exposed to the violence in their home, this affects their school work, their self esteem, they become aggressive themselves. Then poverty comes into play: no money for mothers to leave violent situations. Many families living below the poverty line can't afford extras for their kids and it's hard to meet their needs.

Until we had the hot lunch program, food was a big issue in our school. The kids came, they had nothing to eat, they could not learn, they could not sit in class. We had kids falling asleep on the desk. One child, for example, would get one good meal a day – she would eat here. But she would tell me that they often had just some of those noodles for dinner. It would just be a pack of noodles and that would be it.

Many children are such survivors. They come from homes where their needs are not met, and to a school where teachers have a very unrealistic expectation of them. They say to me, "This child won't listen to me or cooperate." I feel like telling them, "Just be thankful they are here today, considering what they are struggling with every day of their lives."

❖

This worker was young, still full of hope that the system could be changed. She was refreshingly outspoken, her large eyes showed anger, sadness, frustration, yet she wasn't burned out. She was also not scared of rocking the boat. The children obviously came first, not her position. She confirmed, in her honesty, so many items that children have told me about. I can now understand why Patty said a child is not a toy. She surely is speaking from first-hand knowledge of being used as a toy.

Peggie's office was pleasant. Toys were in every corner. She showed me a pile of bags in one corner. She said that it was clean, pressed clothes that she had collected for children who needed them, but the school no longer had room for it.

The Family Advancement Worker program is into its fourth year. It's in twelve schools in Vancouver's inner city. The funding comes from the Ministry of Social Services, through the Family Services Association.

Penny Parry

Penny Parry is the child advocate for the City of Vancouver. She has been studying the issue of equity.

Most people probably think of equity as, well, "let's be fair to everyone," and when you say it that way, everybody thinks, "oh, of course I believe in fairness," and then you say, "well, it's not quite 'equity' as in everybody gets *the same*. It's equity so that everybody has a chance to get to the same place." That might mean that some people get more at the start than others – equity of outcome, not equity of input. So in Vancouver, for example, a good example would be in the west side of Vancouver, families might have a lot of their own money to fundraise for schools. We give exactly the same amount of money to schools, saying, "We've been equitable, we've been fair." Well, no, because the people on one side of the city are able to, in fact, get more resources of their own, so there won't be equity of output. We have to give some people more at the beginning. And when you start talking that way, people get really uncomfortable.

What does that mean for the individual child, though? Say there's little Joey, he's going to an east side school, he's been in foster care, his family is sick. He's starting kindergarten. How do we make him more equal?

Well, for most kids you would assume that a child starting kindergarten is coming having had a good breakfast and Joey hasn't. So maybe in some parts of the city, we need to ensure that those kids have good food. It's not a matter of whether parents want to or not. Some people can't afford it, don't have it, so it might include that.

It might be that Joey comes and he hasn't had as much experience around books or other kinds of things, and people assume that Joey has had that, and unless we help Joey and give him *more* exposure, or show him things differently, he might look like he's not learning as well. And it's not that he can't learn; it's that he hasn't had all of the other experiences.

In other words, equity means some people get more support because they don't have it naturally, and thereby if you put in more support, people will have a chance to have the same outcome.

What are the chances of doing this?

I think the time is right, if you look at the political situation. I still, however, hear people talking about, "It's just a matter of reallocating resources. We don't have any more money." As long as people start by saying that, I think that we'll never get creative about what to do. If people start by saying it can't be done, then we won't do it. But as much as I say that, my experience for many years is that people who are in direct contact with children and youth and family actually have ways and ideas of helping people, and are just sitting there, ready to do it.

What happens to Joey if money and resources aren't available?

Well, then Joey gets blamed because Joey then won't do well in school, for example. So he might start having problems. What ways do children have to show you they're having problems? Well, if you have a choice of being called stupid in school or being a "bad kid," a lot of people choose to be bad, because at least you're in control. At least it gets the attention off the fact that you can't do things. Many of the kids that now get called "conduct disorder" are kids that have had very rough beginnings, who are struggling with a lot of stuff, and who are very angry and have every right to be angry. So Joey gets angry, Joey starts acting out, and then – isn't that interesting – Joey is the problem. And then people say, "You see? Look at the problems that we have in x part of the city." And they not only blame Joey, they blame all those people around Joey. And if we had looked at it in the beginning as, "Hey, what kind of experiences are other people having that give them a different start that Joey doesn't have?" – that could lead to a kind of equity.

Let's say Joey does get some better starts. We know from the literature in the States that you can't just put him in and say, "There you go Joey, you've had a better start. Now just take off and fly." What we need to do is look on the longer term and see, as Joey grows, what else does he need. Otherwise, all the front end won't help if we just drop off.

There's one young person, she could be fifteen, she could be seventeen, anyway, she's very bright. She can articulate herself very well, so it makes me wonder where she came from – she has some good background in terms of books and language. As you look at her, she'll slip into a tough leather, studs, "no shit" stance, but every once in a while you see a very little girl. The thing that is disturbing to me is that there is a little girl out on the street who, to my background in terms of being a psychologist, I think is flipping in and out of reality. One minute she's in, and the next minute . . . That's a young person who's out there with very little help. Youth services are probably the thing that's connecting her to life right now. She's out on the street and squatting in one of the buildings. When you look at someone who is so vulnerable, who is just on the edge . . . one day she'll just move right into the world that she's creating in her fantasy and people won't be able to get at her anymore. That's another reality, but it's not real. When she is into her "no shit" kind of thing, she looks kind of scary, or people will avoid her because she is this dirty little kid. They won't see her vulnerability.

What is your opinion about the services and procedures for children who have been sexually abused?

What you are talking about is the situation where one child who comes from a family that has enough money can go ahead and pay for whatever counselling or whatever help that child needs, and get it very quickly. Another child, whose parents can't afford that, have to wait until their time comes up or when someone can see them. They are delayed an incredibly long time in terms of their needs in counselling. It's another example of inequity at the start, inequity of input. The first thing we should do about it is make more people aware that this is happening because I really don't think people see the differences. They hear about one or two cases and think that they are the exceptions. And what most of us don't see is the devastation that happens, that if you let someone go for a year with no access to getting anything done, you're just building up more and more feelings of helplessness and being a victim and being unable to take control of anything.

I guess just to look at what's important for children, it's

certainly been my experience that the most important thing is that at the right moment, at the right time, somebody is there for you. That doesn't mean that people have to pick the right moment, because they'll never know. It will be the right moment if somebody genuinely cares about these kids. Then they will be there at the right time, because they will have listened to the kids.

I remember recently a young man who had been in care said to me – I asked him, what were the things that helped you live through what you lived through? What he said was, it was the worker who remembered the little conversations he had had, and when it was time for his birthday, the worker brought him a little present. It wasn't fancy. It wasn't big, but showed him that that worker had listened to him, had remembered when he said that he liked football or he liked whatever, and time after time, and young person after young person, and in my own experience, it's been that somebody is there who cares about you and who does . . . what could be a very small thing, but just shows you that they care. I don't think we have a lot of that today. I think that we have people working under very heavy case loads, people working with very big classes, people under all kinds of stress themselves, and they don't have time to listen to kids. So they don't know the kids and so they're not there when it's important.

Georgina Marshall

Georgina Marshall has worked as a welfare advocate for many years. She is a feminist. She is doing a study on child neglect.

❖

Do you think as a society we love our children?

Plain and simple, no. I don't think that we, as a society, love our children. I think that we pretend that we do, and I think that we love certain children. I think we love our own children, some of us, and we love a particular class of child, but we don't love all children, and I think that the proof, the evidence, is in our policies that continually – although they may not be put into place to punish – yet the policies that are put in place continue to punish mothers and children, and fathers. There's forced unemployment, so even when people want to work and want to be independent and try to survive, they can't because of the economic policies. In order for the economy to function as a free market system, there has to always be a certain number of unemployed people. It's harder and harder for people, if they lose their job, they're unemployed for some reason, to get reemployed in a job that provides a living – because the cost of living is just so outrageous these days that you cannot survive as a family on minimum wage.

I think at the institutional level of education, we deal with the issues we've been talking about at an academic level, at a theoretical level. But most of the social workers that I know go into social work because they want to do therapy, individual therapy with people, and that means, by and large, the way the family systems theory goes, you don't pay attention to the structural flaws in our society. You tend to look at the individual and see the flaws within the individual and try to "make that person better." So if a person is poor, if a person is in a violent relationship, if a child is acting out, by and large they are trained to look at that as being the unique, individual pathology. They don't take a look at what's happening in the community, what's happening at a national policy level, that perpetuates those issues.

It's really hard working in anti-poverty stuff, and also working in an organization that gives services to people. People come to us out of desperation, and families would come often with their kids, because they had no childcare. That's an institutional abuse that we're all living with: there is not enough childcare that people can even pay to have, never mind have subsidized. Time and again I would see these people come in, and they're poor and the kids are poor, and I'm so angry that by virtue of where you happen to be born on the status scale, you end up suffering.

It makes me angry and it also makes me sad and I cry fairly regularly because all children have the right to live a decent life, and we are condemning thousands and thousands of children in Vancouver alone to a life of suffering.

People are fed up with the whole "single parent problem." All of these "single mothers having these kids." The reality is, in a patriarchy, and we do live in a patriarchy, the laws are made by men, by and large for the best interests of men. In our patriarchy, when we have children, it's not we men and women who have children; it's women who have children. We are mothers. And even in the best of families, when the father is right in there, gung ho, if you step back and take a look at all of the laws and all of the social policy and all of the welfare laws and regulations, the person responsible for those kids is the mother. All of the research I have been doing around kids who are "neglected," even when there's a father in the family, you read the files, the mother is the one who is blamed for neglecting the kids. There is no exception to that. The mother is the one who is held responsible. So I can't not talk about the issue of children and poverty without looking at the way women are treated as well. Because the system is set up not only to punish kids, but to punish women. We are maintained in a subservient and very unfair position, because we still earn sixty-three, sixty-four cents on the dollar to men. We are at the mercy of all the violence that is around us in our community, that is perpetrated by men. The peacekeepers or the policing people are by and large men.

The way it affects children is that, instead of us being able to get at the issue of poverty and what rights we should be giving children, the way research is done around children and poverty, and the way policy is set up around children and poverty, we always look to the family as a whole and ultimately to the woman, to the mother, as having something wrong with her.

I have been a worker in a transition house. I was for a number of years in the 1970s, and I'm back now, working on a part-time relief basis. It is abominable that, after all these years of the existence of transition houses, it's just as if they had just started up. Kids get yanked out of the family home because the mother is running away from violence and the kids are running away from violence. They get put into a transition house and they're in limbo. Now, maybe a transition house has a counsellor to work with the kids and to help them sort out what's going on in their lives, but maybe they don't. Maybe they have a childcare worker who will work with the kids and let the mom go off and find the housing she needs and go to a lawyer, or do what she needs to do, etc., but maybe the transition house doesn't.

My point is, I don't think it should be the mother and the kids who should be getting out of the house. I think it should be the man who is doing the violent battering. I think there should be an advocate for kids always. There's some semblance of advocacy at some goddamn bureaucratic level, that isn't available to most families, but children need advocates in the community, in the broad geographic community, and certainly in the legal sense.

You seem to be very angry at what the system is doing to children.

I'm angry, yes I am angry, and my anger often turns to tears. In the research that I've been doing on the issue of child neglect, what the research has shown without question is that the most constant and most critical variable in child neglect is poverty. And that is what just blows me away, because every piece of literature you pick up, there may be a researcher trying to point out how bad the mother or father is, but there is poverty, abysmal poverty, and it's the poverty that is hurting those kids. All the social workers know this, who work with poor families, but they can't do anything about it because the policy won't let them give families more money, or help them get jobs.

Patsy

Patsy is a social worker who has worked long and hard in the community. She has always been there for me with a smile, a hug, encouragement. Whenever I was involved with an injustice or a demonstration, over the years, there was Patsy, up front, out front, supporting.

I asked her for some of her gut feelings about child poverty. She sent me the following comments from her heart.

❖

Poverty means hunger, homelessness, wife battering, and child abuse.

A majority of the children who are removed from their families by B.C. social workers are removed due to neglect. What is neglect? There is a direct link between neglect and poverty.

How can a mother who has so little money to care for herself and her children be blamed for neglect? That is exactly what we do – when we pay so little money to families who can hardly find decent housing and money left over for food or clothing, we come along and say that the family is at fault for neglecting the children.

How can we justify separating children from their families, and then pay the foster family three times more to look after the child? Isn't there something really wrong with this kind of thinking?

Yes, I have been a social worker for over twenty-five years. I am also a public servant. So many of us who know the real story are afraid to speak out because of reprisals from our employers and at times from fellow professionals.

It is time that we shouted out to the country as loud as we can that the families need more money and support. Poor families are just as good parents for their children as everyone else, except that the poor need money and support. The majority of the children who are removed from their homes and who are in government care in B.C. should be home with their families. What they need is more money, support, less therapy and counselling. There, I said it!

I will never be able to forget those evenings for months during Expo in Vancouver when the taxpayers' money was used for fireworks. How many thousands of dollars . . . At the same time, the social workers of this province were under pressure from government to save every bit of money in the budget allocated for crisis grants for families. During the same period (it is true today as well) the government has no money to pay for English lessons for a refugee family.

As a visible minority woman I have watched how excuses are used for sexism and racism. In B.C.'s Social Services Ministry there is not one visible minority woman in management. There are over 200 management positions (with a handful of caucasian women) but *one* visible minority man belongs to that group!

Only when there is equality between races, when there is respect for all people regardless of our national, cultural, and income backgrounds could there be justice. When the system excludes subgroups such as cultural or racial minorities, it is obvious that the system is not there for everyone. We have a lot of work to do. The poor and other marginalized groups must work together. Issues are the same!

❖

Patsy mentions that foster families are paid three times what the child's own family is paid to look after him or her. I wanted to investigate this statement, but it's not that easy to do. What I found out is that a family that takes a child in under the Foster Care program is paid $593 a month for a child up to eleven years old, and $684 for a child from age twelve to nineteen. (A family is paid more if it is giving "specialized care," for example to a child who has "mental or physical handicaps or emotional or behavioral problems.")

On the other hand, families receiving income assistance start at a base rate of $963 for a two-person, single-parent family. This includes $520 to cover housing costs, and $443 for support. The support amount increases by $99 for each additional child in the family, while the shelter assistance goes up by decreasing amounts. When there are eight or more people in the family, it rises by $20 for each additional person.

This means that, by the time there are eleven people in the family – that would be one parent and ten children – they are receiving $2055 each month. Yet if these ten children were apprehended by the Ministry of Social Services and placed in foster homes, the government would be paying $5930 *at a minimum* to support the kids! I know this is an extreme example, but it is what the system would do. Wouldn't it make more sense to give the parent the extra money so the family could stay together, and so the parent could maybe be able to afford daycare so he or she could look for a job?

Education

Many of the children and adults that I interview have one thing in common: painful memories of school, teachers, and fellow students. I wanted to find solutions, because this problem has been around for a long time, carried over from one generation to the next. I have heard parents who were poor as children tell how painful school was, and then their children, still poor, feel the judgment of poverty in the school system.

Alicia

Alicia is a second-year teacher from a Vancouver school.

❖

It's a lot easier for teachers to give up on kids that are poor, because they're the ones that a lot of teachers complain, or even not teachers, but the whole system will blame the parents for those kids. They will take one look at their parents and say, that explains why the kid is that way. So everytime you teach them something, they go home and unlearn it, and you just can't get anywhere because every time they go home, it gets undone. That's a very common belief.

Is poverty taught in school at the elementary level?

Taught?! It's not in the curriculum. The curriculum is interpreted any way a teacher wants to interpret it. There's a part of the curriculum that's called social responsibility, and the teachers are required to teach social responsibility, but my view of what teaching social responsibility is is teaching these kinds of things. I've been doing it for two years and dealing with racism, sexism, and poverty directly with these kids. A lot of teachers interpret social responsibility as the children answering teacher-given questions and, basically, the teacher wants the answer that the teacher's looking for, and so if the child gets that answer, then the child is right, but if the child has its own experience, or his own feel of it, then that's the wrong answer.

Kindergarten screening tests give us percentages for each child, of their likelihood for failure in school, their likelihood for success.

Do you mean they come in prejudged?

They come in screened. Based on these standardized tests. And the tests that they use to determine the child's percentage of success, etc., are discriminating against kids that are poor because kids that are poor don't have the same experiences or experiential skills that you learn, for example, if people talk to you, and if people take you to parks and take you to the zoo. You get verbal skills, and you learn how things work, and all that stuff. And just because poor kids fail these tests doesn't mean that they can't learn that stuff. It just means that they haven't experienced it yet, nobody counted from one to ten, nobody took the time to teach them the alphabet. It doesn't mean they can't learn. Maybe the parents are working.

Who benefits the most from these tests?

Kids that have already got the experiences they need to develop those concepts. Middle-class kids. Kids who have had lots of people talk to them, who've had travelling experiences, who have interacted with all sorts of different people and different environments, in parks and zoos, in clubs, in lessons, in those kind of things that cost money. And the kids that have the developmental lag and the experiential lag from not having those experiences, get rated as if they are unable to learn these things. That's not what these tests imply, and that's not what they're supposed to be used for, but as a teacher, you have a new class of kids, and you look down your list and it says that little Eddie has a seventeen percent chance of success, and you automatically go,

"Ohhh, oh dear! Oh little Eddie! What are we going to do about him?" and he senses that, and he already knows there's a problem. And the teacher's and the parent's anxiety about that child doing well translates into his own anxiety about him doing well.

Lorna Bennett

Lorna Bennett, BEd, MEd, a certified school psychologist, definitely wanted to put her name to her interview. Lorna is presently working on a book about women of colour in Canadian society. She is a doctoral student at Simon Fraser University, working on her PhD in structural psychology. She works as a certified psychologist for the North Vancouver School Board.

Many poor children tell me they are picked on by the teachers and classmates because they are poor . . .

I'm not sure if they are picked on because they are poor. I think they are picked on. Their perception is it's because they are poor, but certainly the system, the way it is set up, does not lend itself readily to kids that are poor, because the minute you are poor you come in unprepared academically, you're like, right away behind, because you haven't had the language development, the exposure to books, you probably haven't had somebody that read to you. You probably haven't been to a zoo, to all the activities that enrich kids' lives, and therefore you are behind. You are different, you dress differently, and for those reasons you stand out, and whether you are picked on or not, because of your difference, you perceive things differently. And I think that the way these schools are set up, with the numbers of kids that are in the rooms and the demands on a given person, it is impossible to address that specific kid. I'm not saying that people don't do their best. What I'm saying is, it's impossible to give those particular kids everything they need.

Should poverty be taught in elementary school as a group thing, in a class?

Well, I'm not sure that we need to wait until the kids get to school to talk about poverty. Somehow society owes those kids something, and they should be given a different start from other kids so that when they get there they are at the same place. In other words, they don't have to start behind because they are poor. Society has to address that need. Then perhaps the school could pick up from there to deal with it when necessary, but I don't feel we should wait till they get there to address it.

Given that teachers come from many different backgrounds, is it possible that they knowingly or unknowingly discriminate?

I think it's difficult when you are dealing with a number of kids, a variety of kids, to be what we call "fair" with each kid in exactly the same way. I think that's a challenge. I think teachers try to address that, but I don't think that they always manage to do it. I think that when you are trained, that's the last thing that's talked about. At least in my training I was never taught about somebody being poor, what you say to them. You are taught that kids will be different, that their backgrounds will be different, but you are never taught as far as discrimination. It's not a word we use in education. We talk about minorities, we talk about ethnic groups, but we don't talk about specifics of what that means as far as teaching and classroom interaction. I think it would be fascinating to observe especially what those interactions are. For example, we have done work to look at kids and to see how many times teachers may interact with boys or girls. It would be interesting to see how many times they interact with poor versus middle class. Actually, sometimes when the kids are disadvantaged – as they are often called – they tend to be the kids that are acting out, seeking attention, and because of that they get more attention, but they get it for the wrong reasons. So they call attention to themselves, but it's all negative attention. In essence, they may get themselves out of the room, when they want to be inside the room.

The nice, quiet, polite, middle-class child must be easier for the teacher to deal with?

I'm sure it would be. I often say to kids when I talk to them, if you were a teacher in the room, and there was a kid like you in the room, and there was another kid in the room that's doing what they've been asked to do, which one would you give your attention to? They always say the other kid [the one doing what he or she has been asked to do] because the one that's like they are is being obnoxious.

What about children from minority groups who are poor in the school?

Well, I think that if the average kid is carrying three loads, then these kids are carrying like nine loads. They have to deal with the fact that they are different, they are a visible minority in some cases; they have to deal with the fact that they won't look the same because they can't afford to look the same [in terms of clothing]. Then they have to deal with the fact that they might culturally be different as well. So all those things make them so different that they demand something entirely different from what's being offered. The poverty, the visibility of the minority, and all the other things that may go with it. Poverty means that you come unprepared for what school is all about. I think that their load would be very heavy.

We need to make changes in many ways. The time has arrived when we need two teachers in a classroom. One can no longer do the job and an aide is not good enough.

Poverty and School Performance

by End Legislated Poverty

Introduction

On the evening of March 1 1988, Jean Swanson and Pat Chauncey of End Legislated Poverty (ELP) presented the following brief to the British Columbia Royal Commission on Education. So powerful was their presentation that members of the B.C. Medical Association who were in the room asked them to repeat it at a committee meeting the following week.

The ELP brief placed the abysmal drop-out rate for Canadian schools in the framework of structured injustice in a country where the richest 10 percent of Canadians owned more personal wealth than the other 90 percent of Canadians put together. The Southam Literacy Report (1987) brought to our attention that the overall rate of functional illiteracy in Canada was 24 percent in 1987. What the Southam Report didn't tell us was that the best way to fight illiteracy was to fight poverty. In the words of Carman St. John Hunter, an internationally respected adult educator, "Poverty is the underlying cause of illiteracy. Without any proven will or ability to break the chains of poverty, no government has been able to make significant progress toward universal literacy." ("Myths and Realities of Literacy/Illiteracy" in *Convergence*, Vol. XX, #1, 1987)

The ELP brief warns us that there is a crisis of confidence in our schools and in our society. The school drop-out rate is twice as high among youth from low-income groups as it is among youth from other income groups, and the brief shows us that attempts to remove educational inequalities solely through the school won't work because of the importance of family and community in the process of socialization.

We are not left in despair, however, for the brief makes a clear and succinct statement of what needs to be done in order to restore confidence in our schools and in our country. Changes in the school are suggested, including ways of dealing with cultural difference so that children different from the middle-class norm are not marginalized. At the same time the brief calls for a democratic Canada in which poverty is eliminated. Students will be encouraged to stay in school (or return to school) if they can see that there is meaningful work at decent wages when they graduate, and that they can participate as equals in the life of their own society.

Sandy Cameron, author of "Poverty in B.C."*

❖

Who We Are

We're here today representing End Legislated Poverty, a coalition of nineteen groups concerned about poverty. Most of our member groups represent low income people. We are here because we care about our kids, and we're worried about them.

---

* "Poverty in B.C." is a resource unit sponsored by End Legislated Poverty and published by the British Columbia Teachers' Federation. It was published in 1986, and enjoyed great success across Canada. The Edmonton Catholic School Board copied it, changed the statistics, and produced "Poverty in Alberta." The resource unit is a fact sheet for teachers and community groups about poverty and unemployment in B.C. and Canada, with student activities and resources attached. The sections on children and youth will quickly demonstrate the importance of the subject, especially for young people who are hoping to find decent jobs at decent wages. The National Council of Welfare and the Canadian Council on Social Development publish updated statistics each year, which ensure that the resource unit remains relevant. "Poverty in B.C." fits into the social studies programs for Grades 10, 11, and 12. It is important for students to understand that we live in an economy that creates great poverty alongside great wealth, that poverty is legislated, and that there are many positive things we can do to eliminate poverty in our country.

We believe that we need important changes in our education system, and fundamental changes in our society, if all children, including ours, are to have a decent life.

Our Lives

Many of us live on welfare. Welfare rates are about half the poverty line. It's not enough to live on.

Some of us depend on Unemployment Insurance (UI). UI is 60 percent of wages, but most of us have low wages to begin with. So Unemployment Insurance is not enough to live on.

Most of us work. Perhaps you find that strange, but it is a fact that a growing number of poor people work. We're poor because wages are so low. Minimum wage is only two-thirds of the poverty line for a single person, so if you have a family, your poverty is even more desperate than that. In 1975, the minimum wage level for a single parent with one child stood at 92 percent of the poverty line. By 1985, that level had been reduced to 56 percent (Social Planning Council of Metropolitan Toronto).

Also, many of the new jobs that are being created are part time. Part-time work, especially in the service sector where most of the new jobs are, usually means not enough money to live on.

Housing, even poor housing in basement suites or unsuitable apartments, often takes up 60 percent of more of our income. That leaves very little for food. At times we may have to skimp on housing costs by living in a decrepit neighbourhood, or by sharing a bathroom with strangers, so that we'll have enough money left over to buy food.

Our Children

The most important fact about our kids is that poverty actually kills some of them. Our kids get sick almost twice as often as other kids (1.4 times more for girls and 1.9 times more for boys). They also have almost twice the infant mortality rate as other children.

According to the Ontario Medical Association, poverty is responsible for more lost years of life than cancer. Given these statistics, why is it that cancer is considered a tragedy worthy of much concern and funding while poverty is not?

Very often our kids don't get enough nutritious food. That's one reason why they get sick more and miss more school than other kids.

Our children get sent to the principal's office because they don't bring new running shoes to gym class. But they don't bring running shoes because we, as parents, don't have the money to buy them. There are times when buying those shoes would mean no food at the end of the month.

Our children don't have the same opportunity to exercise their bodies and learn motor skills because they live in apartments with no yards. Frequently, there is little or no privacy to study because the apartment is too small.

Our kids also face a lot of discrimination. Often, they wear second-hand clothes. Because of this, they may be singled out in front of others and criticized for their "untidy appearance." They may be teased or even ostracized by other students.

Kids are quick to learn that poverty is something to be ashamed of. Our kids are embarrassed to be poor, and it's difficult for them to admit to poverty. Powerless to make any changes in the attitudes of our society, our children sometimes direct their anger towards their parents. The loving bond between parent and child can be broken when we, as low-income parents, can't provide the material symbols of nurturing that our society promotes.

Another prejudice that our children have to face is being called "dumb." Low-income kids are commonly perceived in this way. This misconception has meant that more poor kids end up in the slow learner or other "special" classes than other kids. These classes are often a dead end, so our kids end up dropping out of school. Many end up in the illiteracy statistics.

Poverty and Educational Achievement

Numerous studies say that children of low-income families do not do as well in school as children from more affluent homes. A number of theories have attempted to explain this finding. As far as we can tell, the most popular ones see low-income kids as "deprived" or "deficient" in some way.

One theory says that our kids are "genetically deficient" – in other words, that they're born dumb. That's why they do more poorly in school and in life than other children. This theory blames the child.

Another theory says that our kids are "culturally deprived." The idea is that the backgrounds of certain children are so different or lacking that they cannot learn in school. Proponents of this theory point to studies that say poor kids are lacking in primary and secondary linguistic skills because their parents have failed to communicate adequately with them, or have failed to provide enough intellectual stimulation. This theory blames the parents.

Our Position

We agree that poor children often have a difficult time in school. However, we do not agree that this is the result of intellectual, social, or cultural deficits.

The differences in school performance reflect the degree of accommodation that a poor child must make in order to conform to the school's views of what is considered appropriate, normal, or intelligent behaviour.

Our kids are not deficient. They are simply different.

By blaming the parents and children, these deficit theories divert attention from the education system and how it operates to produce certain outcomes, including failure.

These theories can also be self-fulfilling. As teachers, schools, the larger society, and even children and their parents come to believe them, the assumptions behind the theories begin to ensure that the children will not learn. When poor children don't learn, proponents of these deficit theories say their theories have been proved.

In addition to diverting the blame and being self-fulfilling, these deficit theories offer "compensatory education" as the solution to poverty. This includes head-start, pre-kindergarten, cultural enrichment programs, and other special projects which aim at equalizing educational opportunity. What is offered is the attempt to equalize educational opportunity within the school system instead of greater equalization of wealth and power in society. It is well known that attempts to remove educational inequalities solely through the school won't work because of the importance of family and neighbourhood in the process of socialization.

Despite our objections, we are not against compensatory education as long as it is acknowledged that this is an interim measure to the total eradication of poverty. In fact, we've openly supported recent efforts to create a pre-school program in inner city schools. We've also made efforts to introduce an organized food program in Vancouver schools.

However, we feel strongly that this is not enough. These initiatives are only band-aid solutions.

Similarly, other researchers have shown that compensatory education doesn't work very well. Some of the studies concluded that giving money directly to the poor would have accomplished more economic equalization than the educational programs themselves had achieved.

Most researchers ask the wrong questions. They ask, "What is wrong with poor kids? What is wrong with us, their parents, who love them and try our best? What is wrong with our culture?" They call it the culture of poverty or the culture of deprivation.

We know that there are a lot of positive things about our children. Studies show that poor children, while often different from middle-class children, can be independent, spontaneous, creative, open, highly cooperative, and unpretentious.

Poor children show the wonderful human capacity to adapt and cope with their environment, yet it is this behaviour, along with language development, which is so often criticized in low-income children.

So we want to ask different questions such as, "How is the school system failing to serve our kids?" and "How can we change society so that all children can develop to their full potential?"

How the School System Fails to Serve Our Kids

We don't have all the answers, but here are a few of the ways the school system fails our kids:

- failing to provide adequate staff, particularly teachers
- severely restricting lower income students' access to college and university
- maintaining discriminatory attitudes towards poor children which serves to disempower and alienate them

- lack of respect for working class and ethnic values
- absence of programs that confront the problems of racism, sexism, and classism
- culturally biased tests discriminate against our kids, and have served to select them out for sub-standard education and low-status occupations.

Cause for Concern

Studies have found that teacher expectations play a part in the under-achievement of low-income students.

In general, the expectations of teachers and other educational authorities are influenced by race, social class, difference in language habits, behavioural traits, and physical appearance – all of which are culturally defined and very often class-linked. This results in labels and stereotypes which, in turn, contribute to a negative view of the poor.

According to D.P. Hallahan and W.M. Cruickshank, "Many children of culturally different backgrounds are assigned to classes for the mentally retarded, while middle class children exhibiting the same behavioural characteristics are placed in classes for the learning disabled." (*Psychoeducational Foundations of Learning Disabilities*, 1973)

There is a pressing need for in-service training of teachers, principals, and other school board personnel to end discriminatory attitudes and practices toward poor and culturally different children.

To this end, low-income people could be employed to talk to educators about factors in our environment that our children have to deal with, and how these stresses are affecting them. We could show educators how to build on a child's experience rather than attempting to replace it.

Recommendations

- Hire more teachers. This would reduce overcrowding in the classroom and enable teachers to focus on what's good about our children.
- Return family support workers, childcare workers, and other

support staff that were displaced by the Social Credit government's restraint program.*

- Design curriculum so that it conveys a greater respect for the values of working class and ethnic people.
- End student fees.
- Develop programs and curriculum that confront the issues of racism, sexism, and classism.
- Eliminate or minimize selective practices such as tracking or streaming, and the use of standardized tests.
- Demystify the education system to facilitate input from the community into the decision-making process.
- Encourage educators to participate in relevant social, political, and economic issues. This includes support for such social issues as housing, day-care, food programs, and adequate minimum wage and welfare rates.

How We Can Change Society

Part of changing our society involves changing some of its basic assumptions. Education is more than the training of work units. It is the nurturing of citizens for a democracy. We need to recognize the value of unpaid work, both in the home and the community.

Those who do work for pay must be treated as participating human beings, not as commodities to be bought and sold for the lowest wage. This means that young people should be guaranteed decent wages, and women should have equal pay. Workers should have more input into their workplaces.

We need to re-examine our educational tradition. We need to ask ourselves, "Whose interests are being served by the school system?" We need to be clear about the kind of society we want to live in. Only then can we begin to change our schools so they will help our children and ourselves become full citizens in a true democracy.

But changes to the education system will not be enough. If government is serious about improving education, it must take steps to end poverty.

---

* Refers to a mid-1980s program of cutbacks and legislation that lowered living standards and increased poverty for poor and working-class British Columbians.

Why End Poverty?

First of all, poverty denies people the right to participate as equals in their own society. Kids have a hard time learning when they feel left out. Nor can they learn on empty stomachs. They need to have a less stressful home life so that they aren't worrying about paying the bills or getting decent housing. Until our kids can afford to go on field trips or be in sports, they will remain excluded from these activities.

Secondly, our kids must be able to see a decent future for themselves – a future in a stable community with meaningful work at decent wages – a future without poverty.

We believe that the school system should empower our kids to become the policy-making citizens of the future. Learning can be exciting if it leads to control and participation in one's environment. But when classes are so overcrowded that following orders is the only way to prevent chaos, our kids feel that they are being educated to obey, to be followers in our society. They revolt – and drop out.

We suspect that one reason our kids get so rebellious is that they're smart. They can see what's happening. They've experienced in concrete ways the fact that the richest 20 percent of Canadians own 69 percent of Canada's total net wealth, while the poorest 20 percent have less than nothing – minus 0.3 percent of Canada' total net wealth.

Our children see in their own homes how hard it is to be poor. Television, often the only entertainment their parent(s) can afford, pushes them to want what they can never afford to buy. They know that many of their friends and relatives are unemployed or scraping along on welfare. They know that those who are working are still poor. They don't see a very welcoming future.

We Can End Poverty

There is no unwritten law that says that we must have a society which has such disparities in wealth and power. With political will, such inequality can be eliminated.

As parents and government (the government should be our tool, after all) we must work now, not to help a few kids move to a winner spot in an unequal society, but to change our society so that there is a respected place, above poverty, for all children.

Similar calls for government action have come from other members of the End Legislated Poverty Coalition such as the B.C. Teachers' Federation and the Unemployed Teachers' Action Centre. Also, the Vancouver Elementary School Teachers' Association has been supportive of our struggle to end poverty. In 1986, we worked together to produce a resource unit for teachers entitled "Poverty in B.C." Last spring we organized a forum on child poverty, and we are now pushing for a decent, non-discriminatory food program in Vancouver schools.

Ending poverty may seem like an unattainable goal, but it is possible. The first, important step would be to raise the GAIN rate and minimum wage. This would create thousands of jobs. It would increase the provincial government's tax revenue, and it would result in significant savings in health, corrections, and other social service costs. A decline in the illiteracy rate would bring additional savings.

We urge this commission to treat our recommendations seriously. We are sure that our kids would do much better in school if they lived in healthy communities that promised them a decent future, and if they felt that schools were learning places for all children regardless of race, gender, cultural background, and economic status.

Since ELP gave its brief to the B.C. Royal Commission on Education in 1988, other important studies on the connection between poverty and school performance have been published. See *Children, Schools and Poverty* by the Canadian Teachers' Federation in Ottawa (1989). A revised edition of *Children, Schools and Poverty* was produced in 1991 for Campaign 2000. See also *Literacy and Poverty – A View From the Inside* by the National Anti-Poverty Organization in Ottawa (1991).

SCHOOL DROPOUT RATE OF 16 AND 17 YEAR OLDS (Pooled Results for 1982, 1984, 1986, 1987)

	Poor		Non-Poor	
Characteristic	*Rate* %	*Distribution* %	*Rate* %	*Distribution* %
Canada	16	100	8.5	100
Community Size				
100,000 or more	15.2	50.9	7.5	48.6
other urban	18.1	33.2	9.5	32.8
rural	15.5	15.8	9.7	18.6
Weeks Worked*				
0-48 weeks	17.6	67.2	14.3	16.7
49 or more	13.5	32.8	7.8	83.3
Family Type				
couple/children	14.9	46.2	7.6	74.0
female/lone-parent	14.8	34.3	11.5	10.3
other	23.2	19.4	12.9	15.7
Head's Schooling				
0-8 years	21.5	50.7	15.0	42.8
over 8 years	12.8	49.3	6.4	57.2
Spouse's Schooling				
0-8 years	23.9	64.7	15.4	37.8
over 8 years	9.3	35.3	6.1	62.2
Social Assistance†				
yes	21.3	44.8	19.5	4.1
no	13.3	55.2	8.3	95.9

Notes: *Total weeks worked by either or both adults in family.

†"Yes" indicates a family received more than half its income that year from social assistance.

Source: Standing Senate Committee on Social Affairs, Science and Technology, *Children in Poverty*. From data provided by Statistics Canada Survey of Consumer Finances. The survey results do not provide an accurate estimate of the absolute number of dropouts, but they do allow a fairly reliable comparison of dropout rates in poor and non-poor families.

Living and Learning in Poverty

by Ailsa Craig*

Children from poor families are less likely to experience success in our school system than are children coming from more privileged backgrounds. Such children often have two strikes against them before they even start school.

First, they are more likely to have a developmental lag in their physical and/or mental growth. This means they will not as readily master the same skills and concepts as the majority of their age group.

Second, they are more likely to have an experiential lag because of chronic or above-average illness and because of limited access to a variety of enriching cultural experiences. An experiential lag often results in limited vocabulary development, which, in turn, hinders subsequent success in reading.

Upon entering school, disadvantaged children (whose development is already behind their age group) are more likely to suffer from poor nutrition. Some of the behaviours associated with poor nutrition are physical and mental lethargy, retarded mental growth, depression, and hyperactivity. Poorly nourished or hungry children are unable to concentrate; are unable to learn.

Children living below the poverty line are much more likely to come from a family in crisis. The unending stress of having inadequate means to make ends meet results in frustration,

---

* This speech was originally published in the May/June 1987 issue of *B.C. Teacher* magazine. Reprinted with permission of Ailsa Craig.

despair, and a tense home environment. It contributes to marital breakdown, physical and mental health problems, substance abuse, and child abuse. Children from families in crisis bring to school their anger, their frustration, and their pain. They act out, they withdraw, and they more frequently become delinquents. They spend their time trying to get their emotional needs met. Their behaviours limit their own learning, and they also have a negative influence on the learning of others.

More needs to be said about the learning environment. Government restraint has left Vancouver with the largest elementary class sizes in Canada. Some people would have us believe that class size has relatively little effect on learning. Wrong. I have taught for nineteen years. I have taught primary, intermediate, and secondary. I have taught in the rich and the poor areas of Vancouver. Class size has a major impact on learning. The more kids you have, the more time you spend marking, and the less time you have to plan. And, more important, the less time you have to help individual children.

Large classes are particularly damaging for needy children. In schools like Carleton, where I teach, one out of two children is on welfare; the class sizes are at or above the contractual limit. (I have a Grade 5/6 class, by the way, with thirty-three children in it.) The disadvantaged children tend to be concentrated in certain schools.

The present staffing formula in our system is based primarily on numbers, not on need. This ensures that the already disadvantaged child is less likely to succeed academically because there are simply more needs to be met with the same limited resources (i.e. a class of twenty-five in an inner-city school is not the same as a class of twenty-five in another school).

The poor, then, do not have equality of educational opportunity. Restraint* has seriously lowered the quality of education for all of the children in this province. Class sizes have increased, invaluable services have been eliminated, programs have been slashed, and funds for just the basic supplies have dried up. An

* The Social Credit government's restraint program of the mid-1980s. See note on page 140.

example: our school ran out of paper and pencils midway through last year. There aren't enough textbooks to go around. On and on it goes.

Schools throughout the province have been forced to do fundraising to try to cover this government's shortfall in funding. Once again, kids from the poorer schools have been the hardest hit. Our kids at Carleton worked for three weeks on a fundraiser. They worked hard. They raised $4000. A school in a richer area of this city held a casino night and raised $25,000. Another school, also in an affluent neighbourhood, received a $20,000 donation from a parent.

Many schools rely on parental help to cover the deficit in funding. Kids are asked to bring money: money for field trips, workbooks, camping experiences. In poor schools, this is seldom an option. Inadequate government spending, and our present per capita funding formula, both ensure inequality of education for the poor. Restraint increased the number of poor in our schools while vastly increasing their plight. Health care and social workers were reduced, and childcare and family support workers were eliminated, just when kids with poverty-related problems needed them most.

In many schools, lunches left in cloakrooms are pilfered. At Christmas time at Carleton, we collected food for the more needy families in our area. A pitifully small amount accumulated under the tree in the front hallway. One night, kids broke into the school and stole the food from under the tree. They took nothing else, just the food.

While hunger is probably the most dramatic aspect of poverty for these kids, there are many other aspects we have to stop and consider. Here are some I have culled from the journal entries written by children in my classroom.

This from an eleven-year-old girl: "It is not very fun being on welfare. Some people tease you if they find out. When people find out it hurts inside."

From another eleven-year-old: "Poverty is when your clothes get ruined or your runners are too tight, but you can't buy something new. You have to wait till the next cheque comes."

From a thirteen-year-old: "What I hate about welfare is that the money goes so fast."

Another child wrote about a secondary school friend who didn't have a dress for the school dance. The girl's mother sold a dress of her own so that her daughter could have money for one. My pupil wrote of her friend: "She said the day she got the money she felt so guilty."

This from a thirteen-year-old boy: "Living on a low income is very tough, because you worry about things such as bills. Kids worry about that and it's very scary."

From a thirteen-year-old on welfare: "When we have a party I wish I could bring something, but I can't bring stuff to school."

A ten-year-old: "My friend is so poor she picks gum off the ground and eats it. She steals just for food."

And last, a Monday morning journal entry from an eleven-year-old: "We haven't had any food from Friday. The cheque didn't come."

A friend who works in the downtown eastside recently told me of a family whose children had not been at school for three days. He went to the house to check it out. When he reached the house, the father told him that he felt too ashamed to send his children to school hungry, that he'd rather keep them at home hungry.

Limited possibilities, hunger, guilt, pain, fear. This is what the children feel: this is what it means to be a child in poverty. Let's do something about it.

Children On The Street

Michael

Michael is a childcare worker who has been involved in all aspects of childcare for the past twenty-two years.

I arranged to meet him at Carnegie. Some of his ideas and philosophies really pissed me off. Some I felt were right off the wall, but others really made some sense. Michael said that people should have to have a licence to have children, given that we need driving licences, hunting licences, etc. Nobody should start a family until they are trained as a parent. All males should have a vasectomy that could be reversed when they are licensed to have a child.

Michael has worked with street kids and has some really radical ideas about that too.

❖

Street kids are an industry for the sex trade and I think they are an industry for the social service workers. I think we have enculturated the term "street kids," we have made it appropriate for children to go to the street. We have made it an expectation that we will have street kids in our society. Once we do that, and once we create a service around it, we create an industry, and so the industry, once it's created, will not look at what causes it. The people who work with the kids on the street are very quick to blame outside. Well, if you're blaming outside, does that mean you're looking inside? What are we contributing?

I think the solution to street kids does not lie in government, it does not lie in social service, but it lies in how we view children in our culture. We have a myth in our culture that we love and protect children. When was the last time you were in a washroom and saw a toilet low enough for a child to sit on? The concept that we have somehow, that we're a society that cares for and nurtures all its children – even when that's not our practice . . .

You need a licence to hunt, you need a licence to fish, you need a licence to drive a car, you need a licence to sell a piece of real estate, but what you don't need is a licence to have children. There is an assumption in our society that every adult is capable of being a caring and nurturing adult parent. That simply is not true. Until we get rid of the myth that we're a society that loves and takes care and nurtures our children, we are going to have street children. Because it is, what? a god-given right? That no matter who you are, you may have a child? Regardless of what your skill may be or regardless of what the future for that child may be?

It is my belief that everybody, if it is an egalitarian system, regardless of income, regardless of social status, must be licensed to be a parent. In the idea of licensing for children, I believe that there should be a method of birth control that's the least harmful to anybody, and according to all my knowledge up to today, the least harmful and the most reparable would be a vasectomy for males, so that males at birth should have a vasectomy and at a point in time when two people decide they are going to have children, then we can look at the suitability as parents.

Where does poverty fit into your plan?

We don't educate people about the financial obligation of having children. I don't know the figures – you could certainly find it through Stats Canada – that, to raise a child to maturity (which in these days, most children are staying at home till they're twenty-five) costs something like $300,000. So the idea that it's a financial responsibility isn't discussed.

Are you saying people who are poor shouldn't have children?

I'm saying that people in general, poor or rich, shouldn't. If we don't look at the sort of freelance attitude we have towards having children, then the solution for that very clearly is a guaranteed income. If we're a society that loves children and cares about children and knows that children need food and clothing and shelter and to be nurtured and cared for, the only commitment we can make is to a guaranteed annual income.

I believe, if I reflect back on my work, that I'm part of a causal factor that creates street children, because I'm part of a system that is always way behind in terms of cultural and social development. What we began to see perhaps twenty-five years ago, before street children became a phenomenon, is children usually began by running away from something. But at that point, the social structure of the family hadn't changed that much, so children ran away, but they ran back *to* something, to the family. What happened was, eventually running away, within the child welfare system, became a rite of passage – that was something that children did, and was to be expected. Once children began to run away from something, if they couldn't run back to it, for whatever reason, they began to run to something else. So then begins the struggle for the child. They're usually running to a place where there's acceptance for them. Twenty-five years ago I think the field of childcare and child welfare was still built on the social work image of rescuing children. So when these kids began to run *to* something – meaning the street – we weren't aware of what the street was giving them.

When somebody is in danger you protect. There are all kinds of ways to protect. One of the ways to protect is to keep kids away from something that is harming them, to contain kids. You contain kids and you work with them. You don't put them in jail; you put them in places where there are staff and people that can help them.

Detention centres?

No, that's not the model I'm talking about. I'm not talking about putting kids in and punishing them for their behaviour. I'm talking about putting kids in resources that will allow them to deal with their behaviour.

But that's still locking them up!

Call it what you want, I don't think it's locking them up. I think it's embracing them.

Do kids make it?

I've seen or talked to kids that I have worked with. Sometimes they don't function too highly, but they are able at times to break their cycles sporadically. When I see them there's a clear identification that I am a care-giver, or a caretaker.

(Michael had done a lot of work with gay children. We talked about that.)

The issues are power and money and self concept. The power comes from the fact that the most at-risk kids are your gay adolescents. We have a system that I think is just intrinsically homophobic. Gay kids in the system can't come out. How can they come out? How can they get sex? They go downtown. There's two ways you get sex downtown: you buy it or you sell it. And if you don't want to admit what you are, what a great way to disassociate yourself if you've got some man that is willing to pay you. Hey, I'm not gay, I just do this for money. In the sex trade system, the john has all the power. In our culture, a gay adolescent, male or female, cannot go to their peer group for sex. They must go to an adult group.

If a kid is curious, and a kid has a very strong sex drive, they have sex. Are they protected? Is the adult responsible? Most times not. The kid gets AIDS. One boy I know, a fourteen-year-old, self-identified gay kid, came into the system. The invitation to come downtown, the money, the physical attractiveness, the experience was there for him. When he went out, I couldn't give him fifty dollars. I could give him a ten-dollar-a-week allowance. I couldn't give him trendy sport clothes. I could give him a clothing allowance.

The final thing I would like to say is that it is time for people who elect governments – rich, middle-class, and poor people – to really stop looking at the government as being the cause of all ills in our society, and begin to look at what they or we can do as a group of people. Because as long as we see government at fault, we will never look at what we as individuals are doing wrong.

John Turvey

John Turvey works at the Downtown Eastside Youth Activity Society.

❖

Head lice and scabies are commonplace if you work down here. I get scabies once every three years. I get head lice, I guess it's been four years since I had lice. But it's amazing, the social services, working with poor people, those are the kinda things you get. Then, again, as you say Sheila, working with the corporate world, I don't know what you'd take to get rid of some of those parasites. There's nothing available in the drug store for that.

I've been down here thirteen years myself. I keep on saying it was ten years, and then they counted it up, so I've been here a long time. We started our own society because there was virtually nothing available for street youth down here. So DEYAS has been around down here for eight or nine years. For most of that time, I think I made $20,000 a year and the project was me. This year I think we're between three-quarters and one million dollars gross, and we bring about a million dollars a year in social services to the community through our projects.

We have three or four youth workers that just do street work with kids on the street down here – make contact with those kids, try and get them into services, make sure they're safe, stuff like that. Then we've got three youth workers that are called reconnect workers, that do repatriation of kids along with the Ministry of Social Services. What that is, they take referrals from MSS. They identify the kids, get the kids to the airport, on a plane, and returned home – when it's appropriate. Then we have two Latin American street workers. They don't even get out onto the street because they're busy from Monday to Friday, eight to whatever, just doing immigration and income assistance stuff for our growing population of landed Latin American refugees.

We are experiencing about one death a month in the Latin American community, but that doesn't come anywhere close to the deaths of the children and the adult sex trade workers. That's much higher.

I have been told that there are more homeless children and youth. How do you see it?

It's increasing, but I'm not one of these "add water and mix" alarmists. The increase is very gradual, it's incremental, it's slow. The increases for this community . . . the Downtown Eastside gets more the hard-core, entrenched kids. When I use terms like entrenched, that's when kids get more needs met on the street than they would in their family or in their home community. So they develop relationships, they get nurtured, they get their economic needs met, social, personal needs met, all that kind of stuff gets met on the street, and then they are firmly entrenched. So we get a lot of kids like that. We're getting a lot more street people because of the developments on Granville Street, and as that gentrification carries on, you are gong to see more and more of the street population move into the Downtown Eastside. There's a growing population or always has been, of basically white kids that end up – they're the punkers, dropouts, squatters, stuff like that. I think that's where they are looking at putting the safe house in, to address some of the needs for that population. The concern for us in the Downtown Eastside is that most every kid down here has been in care, or does come into care, or is in care of the Ministry of Social Services, and yet we don't have one foster home. We don't have one group home. We don't have one bed in our community, *here,* to place our own children in, even when they come into care. So our kids are placed outside of our community and very often run away from those placements to return to their community and their home. So I'm a bit baffled when all of a sudden the priorities become developing resources for basically special user groups – and they are white user groups. Most of the children down here are aboriginal or non-white. Yet it's easier to place our kids outside of our community and that isn't a priority over things like safe homes for other children, yet we've been screaming for years and years and years down here, but basically it's like screaming into a windstorm.

What would you like to have down here?

We would like to have our own community-based resources for our own children.

What would they be?

We don't know, really. Well, we *do* know, but when you talk about resource development you have to remain fluid. We need a crisis shelter for kids down here, crisis beds. We need a safe home in the sense of, like, today is mardi gras, [welfare] cheque issue day – a lot of kids' parents aren't going to come home. Where do those kids go? And very often those kids end up getting apprehended because their parents get intoxicated or they become dysfunctional when they get money, because of the substance abuse and that. So these kids end up coming into care often, or really get neglected. What we need is safe homes so that when parents blow it, kids can maybe go stay in a safe home for a period of time, while the parents are blowing off steam or indulging themselves in substance abuse or whatever. We need some of those unique initiatives down here.

What about sexually and physically abused children who can't go home?

Then we can develop our own resources. But we want our resources in our community. Why should a child, a kid, have to forfeit their community ties just because they've been a victim of sexual abuse? And that's what happens to kids in this community now. If they're a victim of sexual abuse in the home, they're removed from the home, they're also removed from their community because there are no beds down here for that child. And that's what we would like to see, and those are the priorities in terms of street kids: to keep our children intact, keep them in their own community. Where the other kids that come to this community and end up on the street, that aren't from this community, I think that we have to make all efforts to return them to their own community and their own family.

If they haven't been abused?

That goes without saying. The problem there is, if they can't return them home, very often the resources aren't available in their home community. We can't just, in Vancouver, keep on building short-time bandage resources, when the real need might be in Kelowna or Penticton or Spuzzum or somewhere outside of Vancouver. We could help lobby for more regional development of specialized resources that enable kids to stay basically in the area of their own community. When they become a victim of neglect or abuse in their family, they go into flight, then run to the city; we return them home. They can't go home, but they can at least live somewhere in the area where their community, their friends, their school, their family, and extended family is. It doesn't make sense the way it is now. What happens is, kids come to Vancouver, and very often Vancouver ends up developing the resources because the kids won't return home. Very often some of the reasons they won't return home is there aren't the appropriate or the variety of resources available for the child there, so the child would have a degree of choice when they return to their home community. They might not want to live in Kelowna proper; they might want to live in another community but within the region. So you have to get into that kind of resource development.

Basically, what we've got for street kids is not an awful lot of anything. At last this year we've got an adolescent detox in its first year's operation.

Is it well used?

No, it sits empty sometimes. It's a little more well used than it was, but it's not what we wanted. It's a big, ten-bed, $700,000 resource and what we asked for and wanted were small community-based detox units, with staff and parent models, where they'd maybe take three kids maximum, and deal with them, and be a community base. This detox is based at Sixteenth and Burrard, so for kids from the east side of Vancouver, that's a difficult transition right there. But at least we got something, so in that vein we support it. But we don't support it because we feel that resources for children should be community-based and -operated resources. That's what we're not seeing enough of.

We don't have sexual abuse counsellors in this community. There are no resources available. What victims of sexual abuse have to do now is, you still have to go, lay a charge with the police, get a case number, take the case number to criminal compensation, and they will then pay for your sexual abuse counselling. Christ, it's awful! Why should a child have to go to the police to get counselled because they've been a victim of abuse? What sort of manipulative crap are we allowing our systems to do? We further victimize victims, and then there's not enough staff. What we need are drug and alcohol workers. Our project does not have a youth drugs and alcohol worker. We don't have that so children don't have access to it. The Boys' and Girls' Clubs run our drug and alcohol counsellors and they're not even in this community. So a lot of the resources for children on the streets in the Downtown Eastside are resources that are not even controlled by the community agencies that operate down here.

Do you consider Granville Street to be part of your territory?

No, that's uptown. I think some of the problems in developing services uptown is, some of the agencies up there have not seen that as a community, and so they do traditional interventionist kind of things. One thing about DEYAS is, we're part of the community. We are a community-based agency who deals with kids and other street services. I think a lot of the agencies have always looked at the Granville area as people who *aren't* a community. One thing you have to understand about the street is that it's a community; it meets peoples' needs.

One of the real tragedies around the street is, especially when you look at children that are homeless or adults that are homeless, is our propensity to call people drug addicts or deviants, or labels that allow us to think of them as deviants rather than to think of them as homeless people, victims. Like we'll use homeless as a label with mental health people, but it's very seldom you'll hear anyone call an intravenous-drug-involved person homeless. You'll hear them called junkie, drug addict, and all that. The same thing happens to children on the street. They're called drug addicts rather than children. They're called prostitutes rather than sexually abused kids. So we use all this kind of language to make the position that we leave children in much more acceptable and much more palatable to the middle class. If you drove by children on the street that were being sexually bought and sold, and said, look at those children being sexually procured, or sexually bought and sold by white adult males, and you talked about it that way, rather than looking and saying, oh, look at those hookers! Aren't they young? But calling them hookers, and connoting that they're making free-will decisions as adults, which they're not. They're children. There's a power inequity here.

And children get less protection than what they're entitled to. In the Criminal Code, law 212-4 is a federal law against procuring kids. It's a law to stop kids from being procured into an act of prostitution. There's never been charges laid in all of Canada, and it's been on the books for over five years now. I just wrote another letter to the attorney general's department. I've written articles for five years.

The johns buying children don't get prosecuted?

What the law means is . . . initially 212-4 came in after the law against communication for the purpose of prostitution came in, and it was to control prostitution, a federal law. It's an indictable law, too, so that means you can get five years for it. Basically what the law says is, anybody aiding or abetting a child into an act of prostitution can be convicted of an indictable offence. There've been one or two charges laid in Vancouver, but no convictions. Likewise across Canada. So basically what we've got is like, in cities like Chicago you've got vice cops that present circumstantial evidence to the courts, where the onus to provide evidence is not left to the child. What they say up here is, the child has to testify. That's a dilemma that victims of rape, chilren that have been sexually abused, have always had to bear the burden of providing the evidence as the victim. What they have done in cities like Chicago is, they make their case on circumstantial evidence. What we've basically done in Canada is, we've left the onus for evidence on children, and that's just appalling. So if whoever buys the child on the street is going to get convicted, the very child that he was going to buy has to testify, which we know isn't going to happen and doesn't happen.

Basically, here's the scenario: little Gladys from somewhere in B.C. gets sexually abused at home. The abuse reaches the point that she can't deal with it. There's no resources in her own community, so the child goes into flight or runs from home. School breaks down, her friends break down, her peer groups, she turns to substance abuse to get some kind of solace for the pain. That doesn't work so she leaves her community. She comes to the streets of Vancouver. After a short period of time on the streets, she meets a nice benevolent pimp who takes her under his wing, gets her into a little bit of drugs, but also helps facilitate her entry into being sexually bought and sold on the street. This child is then bought and sold on the street as a commodity. Usually the consumers will be male, white, middle class. The police then will charge her under the law prohibiting communication for the purpose of prostitution. She'll end up in the youth court, charged, and be convicted, and the very men that have been buying her won't be charged. Over 10 percent of your prostitution-related offences against sex trade workers are against children.

So the question is, what sort of message do we give children that end up on the streets by not enforcing this law? The message we give them is: Once you are a sexual person as a child, and once men can perceive you as a sexual entity, then any right for protection in our culture under law is all forfeit. You can be abused and bought and sold at random, and the very laws in place to protect you will not be enforced, and that's what happens. So the message children get is, the laws aren't there. If I'm sexual, my family can abuse me and the abuse will carry on in the street and that's okay. Even the police agree it's okay. Not overtly, but they don't charge the men who buy and sell her. So there's these real tragedies for children that end up on the street, there's those real contradictions in logic and the reality.

How would you handle adults that buy kids for sex?

Adults that buy children on the street . . . you have to understand these are the most vulnerable children in our culture. They are often non-white. They are victims of sexual abuse and neglect. So we have male predators who very often pick kids or young girls who are the same age as their own children. It's really interesting.

People who do this, adult males that buy and sell children on the street – the pimps very often get targeted by our vice squad here, and they've been fairly successful. The consumers of the kids don't get charged. What I think should happen is they should be charged under this law, and they should be sent to jail for two to five years, and I don't care if they sell insurance in North Vancouver and they've got a family and they're established. There's an old saying down here on the street: Do the crime, do the time.

Do you think their names should be published?

Names? Christ! I think photographs! I think this is public information. These are predators. These are the worst kind of predators. These are predators that somehow have an ethical reality where they actually feel, because they have money, that they can exploit poor people and poor children, just because they've got bucks. They're the worst kind of predators, the worst kind of entrepreneurial logic that you've ever heard, where money gives them the right to buy children's bodies and destroy their souls. I say give them five years in prison and let them rot. I don't think you rehabilitate pedophiles. I think you incarcerate pedophiles.

Quest

Quest is an organization that began in 1989. A group of business people felt there was a great need for good, nourishing food served without any hitches, without preaching or prying into people's affairs – a well-balanced, nutritional meal and no questions asked.

We have noticed quite a few children starting to come for food. Why they are coming we don't know. Most of them are with their parents. I don't know if it's more convenient for the mothers to bring them here than to cook a meal. That I don't know because we don't pry, we don't ask questions. I don't know the reasons they come. They certainly are hungry, but most kids are hungry at five o'clock after a long day at school, even if there's lots of food at home. They eat a good, hearty supper at most times.

We have seen more and more coming. The odd time children by themselves are coming. Quite a few punkers and people that we hear are sleeping in the parks, who are not on any type of social assistance. They come here in great numbers, maybe fifty to sixty every night.

What kind of an increase have you seen in the number of youths, under twenty-one?

Fourfold.

What makes your food different?

We always have salad. We always have fruit. We always have a main course. We serve it with dignity. We don't preach or pry. We don't have a sermon. We don't tell them they shouldn't be here, or that we're just doing this because nobody else will look after them, which is the message they get from a lot of other organizations. It's also good food because we have a lot of support from the food industry. We're getting a lot of help from private citizens and major corporations, like bread and muffins from Pilsbury batter. All workers are volunteers. In fact, all of them are on welfare. Most of them, or all of them, came to us for a free meal, got the meal, and felt that they wanted to help, and they've stayed on. When we do dinners here, we have anywhere from fifteen to twenty of them that are helping us. None of them are paid. And, well, I started off with a bunch of them at seven o'clock this morning. That's when we started, and we probably won't finish till eight, eight-thirty, nine, so that's like a fourteen hour day and they're not being paid for it.

(I struggled with his comments about mothers finding it more convenient not to cook a meal. I pointed out to him that they were there because they were poor and hungry, not out of convenience.)

Betty McPhee

Crabtree Corners, right in the middle of the Downtown Eastside, has a daycare, a drop-in for women, with food and a shower, and clean clothes. Alcohol, drug, and narcotic recovery groups meet there. There are outreach workers; they work with babies who have been born with fetal alcohol syndrome. When you go in there's the smell of soup cooking, boxes of donated clothing, chesterfields with women sleeping on them, women busy making soup and bannock. The centre is small but well used. The daycare is on the other side of the building and that's well used too.

Betty McPhee is the director of Crabtree. She is really laid back, and her office, which is small, has all kinds of stuff that is needed by the users of Crabtree, from toys to hats to books, sweaters, and various files, and a couple of shabby chairs. Betty is always there to give me a hug and encouragement, but there's no b.s. from her, ever!

❖

Recently we had a fourteen-year-old girl who had run away from home because of repeated sexual abuse. She was brought in by an older woman sex trade worker who was trying desperately to get services for this fourteen-year-old. There was no safe housing for her, she wasn't eligible for welfare, and the older woman knew it was just a matter of time, if she didn't get the services, before that young kid would end up being a sex trade worker herself, and as it stands now, there are no real safe houses for these children and it has to happen. It was tragic.

You have a fourteen-year-old girl who doesn't want to go into foster care, is scared to go home because of abuse. It's closing time, where can you send her?

Well, the problem is, she was afraid to go to the ministry. She was afraid that if she went to the Ministry of Social Services, she would be sent back home or that she would be sent to a group home, and she'd had bad experiences there, so there really isn't very many places to send her. This is all too common. What we can do is supply very small band-aids. We can feed them, we can feed the young kids, we can provide them with referrals to the street nurses, we can give them clothing, but it's not enough.

Do a lot of these children finish up in prostitution or pushing drugs to survive? If they can't get money from welfare, how do they survive?

If there isn't some sort of intervention, and there usually isn't, they end up prostituting, getting involved with street activities which include alcohol and drugs, and many of these kids end up extremely battered, and by the time they hit their twenties, they're very high risk for HIV and for battering. I feel such rage at the system that allows these children to be throwaway children.

In terms of practical solutions, we have to start very very early. We have to provide single parents with adequate income to feed and clothe their children, to provide them with the same things that middle-class children have, so that by the time they enter the school system they are on an equal footing. It's been my experience that many of the children that are classified as developmentally delayed in our daycare, this is directly attributable to poverty. They're growing up in hotels, in substandard housing, they're sharing suites with two or three families. In the hotels there are often shooting galleries [for drugs], unsafe places for the children. There is no intellectual stimulation for these kids, so of course they are going to have developmental delays.

The solution has to . . . children *have* to become a priority.

One of the problems that we see is an ongoing issue with poverty where the children are hungry. The third week of any welfare cheque month, parents run out of money for food, run out of money for formula, run out of money for diapers. These children can then easily be seen as neglected, which is not the case at all. The parents do the very best they can.

If a safe house were set up, how do you think it should be? What should it be like?

First, what I would like to see, because I work with children from six weeks of age up to their sixth birthday – and last year there was 456 children that we saw – I would like to see a 24-hour emergency daycare, or a safe house, where those children could go and be safe and have adequate care for a few days. I think that would prevent a great deal of apprehensions.

Amongst the middle class, when somebody gets a bonus, they can go off to Harrison Hot Springs, and they can hire a babysitter to look after their kids, but amongst the poor, they have to get someone to look after the kids who sometimes is not as reliable as they should be, and that's where a lot of difficulty happens, a lot of abuse happens. I think a 24-hour shelter, with properly trained staff, would really help that. Amongst the teenagers there have to be safe houses for the children as well, and again, I think there should be support staffing in those houses for those kids.

A wonderful example of a community response to child poverty was the Child Poverty Action Group: a small group met at Crabtree over a period of time and fought to get lunches into the inner city schools. It was a *long* battle. I think those women are extremely courageous. They all had experienced what it was to have poverty in their lives, and their children's poverty. Finally this is happening in twelve schools now, so it shows what a few women can do. There currently is a buzz phrase: equity of outcome. What that means is, the children on the east side and northeast side of Vancouver should have equal access to services as the children on the west side, the middle class and the upper class. This is not true today; we don't have the same amount of speech pathologists, psychologists for children. All of the services are not equal to those on the west side according to the population and according to the need. That also has to change, and it's my understanding that the child advocate of the city of Vancouver is working this year to try and make a dent in that.

Maggie Duckett

Maggie Duckett has been involved with Gordon House Youth Works for the last four years. A warm, friendly, Australian woman, quite small, she has a loving but don't-mess-with-me attitude.

What can you do for children who are under sixteen? What do you do?

If they're not prepared to go to a ministry office, for instance, to the Adolescent Services Unit, there's very little we can do. There really are not provisions. These kids potentially are going to be apprehended by the police, who are doing constant surveillance of who's on the street.

Street Youth Services, which is a multi-funded organization downstairs from us, they work with anybody and everybody who's on the street in this general area. Their primary mandate is to alert those people who are on the street of what services are available for them, to provide an environment where they can come in for counselling when there's no ministerial resources. An eleven-year-old could come in to Street Youth Services and the staff would try to assist them to get into some kind of safe environment.

We've been very fortunate that we receive donations of bread and coffee and those kinds of things. We don't feed them a nutritional meal; we don't have a budget to do that. We give them something warm and filling.

This program [the Gordon House Youth Works] is successful

because we offer a very supportive environment, we offer very practical programming. The focus of this program is to help those trainees who want to become employable, to become employable. We have group discussion, classroom-type discussion, information, some of the information we give is more in a literary form, but in the general discussions, questions and answers, sharing of experience, provision of information, we alert our trainees to all the resources that are available.

The training allowance is $5.50 an hour for all activities within the program. So for the sixteen weeks the trainees are active in the program, no matter what activity they're participating in – they could be at a host employer getting work experience, they could be in a classroom environment, they could be out doing information interviews – as long as it's a program activity, they'll get $5.50 an hour.

I'll tell you a success story about Alice. Alice came into the program very much a street kid, was living in a squat. An intelligent girl, has Grade 12 – which is quite unusual; most of our target group have considerably less education – very environmentally aware, but very resistant. Alice had a lot of difficulty getting onto social assistance. She was eighteen, so she certainly was of an age. She had come to Vancouver, she had no means of support, she had one change of clothes. She was very resistant to authority. Her life experiences had been very very negative. She had been in and out of various schools. As I say, she was intelligent and she had completed Grade 12, but she had no idea of where she wanted to go. She was really down, very poor self esteem, no self confidence, just generally at loggerheads with everything that was going on in the world. She came into the program and for the first three or four weeks expressed a lot of resentment, had a lot of trouble coping with the structure of the program. However, at about the four-week level she seemed to come to terms with the fact that if she was going to achieve what she wanted to achieve, the changes had to come from her. We were providing an environment for change, but she was the one that had to make the changes. So she did a complete turnaround in her attitude. She was placed with a host employer, in an environmental organization. That really was the significant turning point. She became very much involved with this organization, she did a lot of volunteer work out of hours so that, even though she was getting paid $5.50 an hour for the specific time, she did a lot more. As a result of her real interest and the fact that she had presented herself so well to this organization, and become invaluable, she, with their support, wrote a proposal for funding in order to create a job opportunity for herself within that organization. The proposal was accepted, she has been hired, and she is one of the key people in that organization now and is doing incredibly well. As a result of being employed, she's been in a position to be a supervisor host employer for another trainee that's active in the program.

Does anybody get to your heart?

Most of them get to your heart. There are very few that don't. I'm one of the only smokers on staff and that gives me a little status with the kids because they all smoke. We sit downstairs and talk. I make it very clear to the kids that when I deal with them, I'm dealing with them as adults, not as victims of abuse. I have a twenty-year-old of my own and I have explained to the kids here that the way I see them is exactly the same way I can see my own twenty-year-old and his friends, and I treat them the same way. I really sometimes have to sort of close my mouth not to be a mother.

If you had the power to make some changes, what would they be?

One of the things that I would do would be to put something in the water that automatically prevents pregnancy, so that if somebody decided they wished to have children, they would have to take medication in order to be fertile.

The next thing would be that every child, when they enter school, from the day they enter school, would have access to a child counsellor, and that child counsellor would be a support through no matter what, and would have the power to intervene at any point, with the school, with home, wherever. That person would be there for the child. They would have the power to say, this child is not learning effectively. We must find out why, we must change the environment for that child, so that the learning opportunity is there and is equal, no matter what.

I find it quite terrifying the number of children, young adults, who come through this program, whose level of education is at maybe a Grade 6. They are capable of learning; the problem is that they don't have learning disabilities, but they have been in a very negative home environment, school environment, whatever the circumstances, the learning process has been disrupted because of the social things in their lives. I think that there are two major breeding grounds for street kids. One is the home environment from early childhood, where there's been sexual abuse, where there's been alcoholism in the family, where there's been neglect of the child. And that neglect translates to the child as, "Nobody cares about me." So there is nobody acting as a positive, caring advocate for that child. The child then moves into, "I have to do it myself," and the only way they see to do it for themselves is to behave negatively in order to get attention.

I would like to see my tax dollars – and when I say my tax dollars, I mean me and everybody else who has a child, who has anything to do with children – for those tax dollars to be priorized for services to children.

There are very few free services. Once a child gets to be nineteen, the free services are almost non-existent. And the waiting lists are horrendous. Children are waiting for housing, they're waiting for assessments, they're waiting for counselling, they're waiting for treatment. They're waiting because there are so few resources available because the government sees fit to put its funding somewhere else. This is an ongoing problem, and it's becoming worse and worse and worse every year. The government talks constantly about provision of services, but we see nothing.

The fastest way for either a juvenile or an adult to receive services is to break the law and be apprehended. It is a horrifying truth that, once you're in the criminal justice system, you will receive a lot more services than you would have if you were not in the criminal justice service.

Child Poverty: Making the Connections

by Linda Marcotte

In looking at the issue of child poverty I will be using the three steps of popular education as a model: 1) starting from people's personal experience; 2) deepening the analysis of this experience; and 3) moving to action. I will be starting with my own and my children's experience of poverty, deepening the analysis of the causes of poverty with the information I learned working with End Legislated Poverty, and I will end with examples of action we can take to end child and adult poverty. Child poverty is the result of adult poverty so I will be using those terms interchangeably.

I developed the following ideas about child poverty from my own experience of growing up white in the poorest family in our neighbourhood, a mixed rural/suburb on the outskirts of Ottawa in the 1950s and 60s. In the 1970s I was a working poor person in Calgary, Alberta, Alma, Québec and White Rock, B.C., where I was a student and worked in restaurants washing dishes, bussing, and waitressing. I raised my two children on welfare on my own, beginning in 1978, when Steven and Melanie were two and four years old, to 1989. I've worked at End Legislated Poverty as an organizer since 1989.

End Legislated Poverty (ELP)

End Legislated Poverty is a coalition of twenty-eight B.C. groups that has been organizing to end poverty since 1985. We help low-income people and their allies to get organized. We do research. ELP has ongoing campaigns to raise welfare rates to the poverty line and the minimum wage to 122 percent of the poverty line. B.C.'s minimum wage in 1975 was 122 percent of the poverty line. Today (September 1992) the minimum wage would be $9.05 an hour if it was 122 percent of the poverty line. I'll be saying more about our other campaigns shortly.

A Word About Privilege

With the exception of a seven-month teaching job in 1974, I have been poor most of my life. This was painful and hard. I was politicized early, but my analysis of my own and my children's poverty experience is largely a result of my present privilege of getting regular, decent wages. This has given me the advantage of having the time, energy, and money to buy books and magazines, to read and to think. Sharing information and talking with other low-income people and anti-poverty workers across Canada and from other countries is a privilege that comes from my work. Part of my ELP work is to write, so I have the time to think and develop my ideas. Through the training and support of the other ELP workers and low-income people who work with us, I'm aware of and overcoming low self esteem and feelings of worthlessness and powerlessness. These feelings are a result of internalizing the oppression that came from being a poor woman.

Classism and Child Poverty

The pressure to change myself and look for ways to work with other people to change the world came about because of my children. I saw them being hurt and defeated by poverty. They didn't get the things other children around them took for granted: family cars, extravagant birthday parties, lessons, sports, vacations, stylish clothes, their own room, a quiet place to do homework, a yard with their own play equipment, expensive toys, eating out in restaurants. It hurt me to see them being hurt by classism, that our family wasn't "normal." "You mean you don't have a Dad *or* a car?" was a question other kids often asked.

I saw them being defeated by the educational system where the insensitivity of the teachers and principals about single parent families and poverty made them feel ashamed of themselves and our family. Schools' promotion of values like competition, authoritarianism, and "making square pegs fit into round holes" hurt Steven and Melanie, and hurts other kids, poor kids, disabled kids, kids coming from families who aren't white, Anglo-Saxon, Christian, or heterosexual.

Here are some of my memories of mothering in poverty:

- the kids always having stained, patched, or out of fashion clothes;
- sending them to school with plain, unexciting lunches every day;
- no hotdog or donut treats at school fundraising day;
- no cable TV, actually no TV for five years. I put it away so they wouldn't want what I couldn't buy them;
- no movies;
- arriving places tired from carrying stuff and worn out from waiting in the cold or wet or hot (depending on the weather), rumpled, dirtier from riding the bus than getting around by car;
- shame in inviting kids over. "Where's the couch?" "Where's your stereo?" "Where's your room?" were the kinds of questions from these young visitors;
- birthday parties – kids asking, "Is *this* all there is?"
- saying NO to Steven and Melanie all the time;
- me worrying and anxious about money. "Will we make it to cheque day?" Me being scared anything will happen that costs anything. This fear taking energy away from living, having fun, and paying attention to the children;
- dragging the kids and two garbage bags full of dirty laundry on the bus every week to do laundry;
- always looking for money or returnable bottles on the ground;
- me escaping into reading or watching TV;
- being constantly worried they weren't getting enough nutritious food to grow and be healthy;
- being homeless for four months and living with friends and at two different friends' houses while they were away, with our things stored on another friend's back porch;
- being aware of how out of their peers' culture and experience my children were, but powerless to do anything about it.

We have been lucky to live in a housing co-op since 1982 and the happier memories are:

- co-operating with other low-income people in the housing co-op for money, food, and clothes;
- caring for each others' children;
- Steven comparing birthday gifts he got from well-off friend and from low-income friend. "The first one must like me better – the present is nicer." And us talking about money and friendship;
- coming over with extra homemade soup or bread to share, loving the pleasure of sharing;
- a joke at the White Rock Women's Place: "Send Linda to any conference or meeting so long as there is free childcare she'll go willingly!" because I needed a break;
- going into the welfare office with each other;
- laughing at our extravagant problems together instead of despairing alone.

In spite of the good times and the lessons about the co-operative, resilient, strong, and dignified spirit of working-class and low-income people I've learned, it hurts me to remember these times. I feel bad for what my children felt and how they struggle now with the effects of all those years. Writing this brings tears to my eyes. I feel bad because I had to bring my children up in poverty.

I wanted the world to change for Steven and Melanie. The low-income adults I knew had suffered *enough* shame, poor health, unrealized creativity and happiness, shortened lives and dreams. I did not want my kids to be cheated as well. It only made perfect sense to put my whole self, as shaky and flawed as that felt, to work to make things better for them.

My Politicization

Changes in my thinking about poverty came slowly. Moving from judging and blaming the "victim"/myself attitude was difficult. I must have tried every way anybody's thought of to get off welfare: therapy, back to waitressing, job training, more education, budgeting and courses on stretching your dollar (or

"1000 ways to use hamburger"), assertiveness training, a course on how to dress and wear makeup, getting boyfriends and roommates.

A turning point came when my wallet was stolen in Vancouver in 1981. When I reported the theft, the police insisted I had to submit to a lie-detector test because I was on welfare. I was outraged at this policy and contacted a friend who was teaching me how to be a welfare advocate. Reporters wrote stories in the newspapers and other people came forward to say it had happened to them. The issue was brought up in the legislature by Rosemary Brown, MLA, and the Vancouver Police policy was changed.

Thinking of myself as a feminist in the early 1980s was an important step. I took the idea of the personal being political, and the political being personal to heart. Having a mentally disabled child forced me to ask the question, "what is normal?" Training to be an advocate for people on welfare taught me about our rights as poor people. Standing up for other low-income mothers and their children made me see I could be strong and change the seemingly unchangeable in the Ministry of Social Services bureaucracy. I made friends with other anti-poverty activists, and when I started thinking about myself as one of them, I knew I could never go back to being a single mom on welfare without working for economic and social change.

Reading about poverty, getting information from alternative sources, and studying the history of liberation struggles, put my search for pride, self esteem, and justice in context. Seeking out the people, the music, literature, and art of other than white, English-speaking Canadian cultures helped me question my idea of reality. I began to wonder, "Is the way things are, the way things have to be?"

Being on welfare was bad, but another low-income woman and I realized while talking one day that we were the first generation of mothers who didn't have to stay with abusive husbands to survive. If a man died or left us, we didn't have to link up with another man if we didn't want to. We could raise our children on welfare, although only between 40 and 60 percent of the poverty line. Welfare enabled us to choose to stay home and mother our children without abusive partners.

Compare this to Mexico. In 1991, when I talked with Regina Avalos Castaneda, an organizer for food for impoverished mothers and children in Mexico City, she told me, "There's no welfare here . . . [as a mother] you stay with a man who helps support you, you work selling things in the street, you work on the streets selling yourself."

Global Analysis

Just a word about this next part. This is a very complex subject; whole books are written about each of the components of the structural adjustment programs. (See notes on SAPs on page 178.)

I began to understand how poverty is deliberately created in Canada and around the world. Big business representatives and lobby groups that represent them have been asking governments for changes that benefit themselves and the wealthy people they represent. Socialist economists name this the corporate or neo-conservative agenda. These requests, accompanied with generous donations to the politicians who listen and act on them, are being made to "keep the country competitive in the global market."

Linda McQuaig, in her 1991 book *The Quick and the Dead*, says it well, "But what foreign investors deem to be important is, needless to say, often very different from what a country's population considers important. A low infant mortality rate, clean environment or a equitable distribution of the country's resources may be pleasing to the bulk of the population, but does little to boost a country's rating in the eyes of international investors. On the other hand, high interest rates and low government spending might bring hardship for the majority of the population, while attracting foreign investors in droves."

We will be sharing more and more of this "globalization of poverty" if the corporate lobby groups and our governments keep having their way. In Canada, the result of these policy changes has been having an official unemployment rate of 11.6 percent be seen as normal, a shift from full-time to part-time jobs, a shift to more jobs in the low-paying service sector, more people on UI, more people on welfare, more homeless people – more people including children, living in poverty.

More children are hurting and dying, here in Canada and

worldwide, as a result of wealthy people using government to change economic structures for their own benefit.

People working with ELP have learned so much as we organize people to action against poverty. When we low-income people have information about the real causes of poverty, we can see we're not to blame for our situation. Even if we *could* stop smoking or go back to school or be "better people" somehow, poverty is a product of our system. People start to feel stronger, a weight of guilt and shame is lifted from our shoulders, and there is room for righteous anger. The hopelessness and powerlessness that I carried around like an old winter coat fell away. What replaced it? Fury about injustice, and passion to liberate myself and all low-income people from it.

Using researching methods based on popular education models, ELP changed how the economy can be studied. Instead of being too overwhelming, confusing, and complex, ELP's three-hour workshop called "Understanding the Corporate Agenda" has participants leaving with a grasp on the way the economic system works. The participants say they know which groups benefit and which groups lose from recent government policy decisions. They have some ideas about actions they can take to end poverty. And workshop participants feel empowered individually and as a group to act.

Now, let me describe two ELP campaigns for justice for low-income families.

School Lunch Programs

I have been working to organize low-income people and their supporters about child hunger and the need for school lunch programs since before I started working as a paid ELP staffperson. End Legislated Poverty brought the issue of child poverty to the public attention in Canada when we started to work for lunch programs in Vancouver in 1987.

The ELP coalition brought together representatives from teachers, public health workers, churches, parents' groups, unions, social workers, and the Vancouver School Board to plan a child poverty forum in April 1987. Two-hundred people attended. One of the recommendations was to work on getting hot, non-stigmatizing lunches in the poorest schools. We organized groups in Vancouver, Victoria, Nanaimo, Surrey, and Burnaby. Children came with us as part of the delegations to the school boards and city councils.

Always making poverty a political issue and not an individual problem, ELP said school lunches were needed because the welfare rates and minimum wage were unlivable, rents were too high, and there was a terrible lack of decent jobs at decent wages, cheap, reliable childcare, and non-profit social housing.

We said politicians could do something to correct all these barriers to good child nutrition and health, but they were choosing not to. Poverty and child hunger is legislated. The only thing needed to end child poverty and hunger for ever was political will.

When we got comments that blamed low-income people for their poverty, or arguments for charitable programs, we persistently said the politicians could do something concrete to help children stay healthy, learn better, and stay in school longer – by putting some money aside to pay for lunch programs.

We worked hard, we had fun, and we won! In January 1992, the new NDP government in B.C. announced a $7 million fund to feed kids school meals. In June, $11.6 million more was announced. There are school lunch organizers in Edmonton, Toronto, and Montreal. New Brunswick just had a Royal Commission that recommended nutrition programs in that province because thousands of children are going to school hungry. It's great to think of all the thousands of children who are eating lunches at school or who will be in the future as a result of our work. We started a movement!

Ending Forced Employment

The lunch program work was a pro-active anti-poverty campaign that low-income women with ELP initiated. ELP also does organizing work that is reactive. An excellent example of this is the fight against the $50 a month cut in welfare benefits for single parent mothers in 1989. It took nine months for the Social Credit provincial government to back down and give the money back. Another big victory! But the legislation related to the $50 cut that forced single mothers on welfare to look for work outside their homes when their youngest child turned six months did not change.

ELP worked with single mothers on welfare affected by this legislation to raise the issue, plan demonstrations, and lobby government to change the law. In December 1991 the new NDP government announced the change. B.C. went from being the province with the most repressive welfare law on this issue to being the best in North America – mothers on welfare could wait until their youngest child turned nineteen years old to look for work outside their homes. Victory in this campaign affected 40,000 single mothers and their kids.

Charity And Poverty

Charity as the solution to poverty is as old as institutional religion. Today, big business and government are pushing charity as never before. Instead of addressing the unequal distribution of wealth and power, people are encouraged to feel generous by giving their leftovers to poor people. Peoples' generosity and need to help others is manipulated. Children are exploited so the public eye is off the creators of poverty – the government and big business. Poverty is made to look like the individual's problem. Children are shown in newspapers and TV as innocent victims of forces out of human control.

The Political is the Personal

Travel on the bus and hear kids being yelled at, hit, manipulated, threatened, stared at, humiliated, embarrassed. Walk into a classroom and see kids humiliated, put down, patronized, hurried, controlled, bored, and forced/encouraged to compete against each other. Children in general are not treated well here in Canada. Working-class and low-income children have life even rougher. Around the world, in poorer countries a child's life can be hell.

From Dave Todd's Vancouver *Sun* newspaper series in July 1992 on worldwide child labour: "Here are little children, who would be in school, making clothes for distant consumers, among them little American, Canadian, and European children their own age."

"The overriding truth is that child labour causes and perpetuates poverty," Bob Senser (human rights director of the AFL-CIO Asian-American Free Labour Institute in Washington) says, and the West's tolerance of the practice is part of a "chain of irresponsibility" that starts in the sweatshops of Dhaka and ends in North America's air-conditioned shopping malls. "At no point in the chain does anybody in a position of economic power or authority do anything to look after these children's interest."

The connection between how we think, and what we think about, how we feel, what we do, and the corporate or neo-conservative agenda, is so close it's hard to think about. The day-to-day struggles families work through make us just reactors to the changes in the economy, not the actors we should be. We try to deal with the consequences of this agenda, and The Big Picture seems to happen somewhere out there without us.

Newspapers and magazines cost money and don't get to the depth of the issues. With most of the media owned by the very people pushing the neo-conservative agenda it's hard to get real information about real people's lives. All around, the corporate message is like the air we breathe. "Don't question authority. If you're not well off you're a loser. Compete to get ahead. Have a drink. Buy, buy, buy."

And it's *in* us as well, in the form of consumerism, competition, organizing hierarchies and obeying authority without question. The neo-conservative agenda is in us as internalized oppression if you're from one or more of the loser groups (aboriginal, low income, working class, women, person of colour, old, disabled, not heterosexual) or as internalized privilege if you come from one or more of the groups with power and privilege (male, middle class or wealthy, able bodied, young but not too young, heterosexual, white).

Most people in Canada are combinations of these two, with each one of us internalizing our oppression and privilege. We're only just beginning to think about, talk about, and work on acknowledging our differences, using our strengths and skills from our privilege, and hearing each other talk about the pain oppressing each other has caused.

How do we all work together to end poverty and have social and economic justice?

- let yourself care;

- notice when you feel different, left out, not listened to or heard, and talk to a friend in similar circumstances;
- think of everything in your life as both personal and political;
- start thinking of children as our collective responsibility, not their parents' property;
- seek out and read alternative newspapers, from the anti-poverty, aboriginal, women's, environmental, and peace communities;
- listen to alternative radio stations;
- contribute financially, if you can, to groups that are helping to make legislative, structural changes to help ordinary people;
- if you have privilege, say as a teacher or lawyer, use your resources to give low-income people access to what they need;
- call ELP and groups working for social and economic justice for people in Canada and worldwide for more ideas;
- work with us.

Will we end poverty? "When [we] have a clear agenda that is unsanitized and unapologetic, a mobilized mass that is forceful and public, and a conviction that is uncompromising and relentless" (Susan Faludi, *Backlash*). Where do you see yourself in this work?

I thank the End Legislated Poverty staff of Patricia Chauncey, Pam Fleming, and Jean Swanson; ELP's Charity Project workers; people who are doing popular education; Campaign 2000, a national coalition of groups lobbying for the end of child poverty by the year 2000; Regina Avalos Castaneda, Dave Todd, Linda McQuaig, Ken Battle, and the Caledon Institute of Social Policy; Susan Faludi for her book Backlash: The Undeclared War Against American Women*; and all my friends for helping me write this article.*

Some Notes on Structural Adjustment Programs

Programs that structurally adjust national economies (SAPs) include:

- "tax reform": lower taxes for corporations and wealthy people, and higher taxes for low- and middle-income earners;
- privatization: selling government services to businesses to make a profit, and giving private businesses the right to manage investment, energy, the environment, wages, health and education, culture, and resources;
- high interest rates;
- free trade deals with other countries;
- "a new labour market strategy" designed to "increase the flexibility of the workforce," increase low-wage, part-time, and contract employment, and reduce the strength of organized labour;
- cuts to federal spending;
- union busting.

The Canadian federal government has been putting SAPs in place by:

- signing the Free Trade deal with the U.S. and, now, Mexico;
- deregulating energy;
- implementing drastic tax changes, increasing the burden on low-income, working, and middle-income people and taking it off wealthy people and corporations;
- privatizing over twenty public firms, including Air Canada and Petro-Canada;
- cutting federal spending, including reducing transfer payments in education, health, and social services to the provinces, forcing them to 1) raise provincial taxes, and/or 2) borrow more abroad, and/or 3) cut spending in health, welfare, and education, and/or 4) privatize;
- cutting unemployment insurance and social assistance;

- replacing the federal sales tax with the more regressive GST;
- maintaining high interest rates: ostensibly to control inflation but in reality aimed at reducing domestic demand and attracting capital from abroad to offset Canada's international debt service payments.

Other Issues Affecting Children

Child Labour

Often today, young people in high school must work if they are to be able to afford university or college tuition fees. Ironically, as a report by Maureen Baker points out, "adolescents are able to find only low-paid service, clerical or manual labour jobs . . . part-time during evenings and weekends. Their jobs enabled them to afford an education yet cut into their time for homework and extra-curricular activities."

I was told that the food industry uses permits to hire thirteen- to fifteen-year-old kids in B.C. An example would be A&W, which hires quite a few children under fifteen years old. These children are paid a lower minimum wage than adults receive for the same amount of work. If a child were independent and living alone, this wage could never pay for rent or buy enough food for a month.

The question is, are the food corporations using children for cheap labour, with nothing but minimum wage and layoffs at age sixteen to look forward to? Or is it good, as some say, for children to be in the real world of the work force? Some children who start work at thirteen may rise to become manager in a fast-food franchise. I don't know how often this happens, and I don't know the answer to my questions.

Another report, by Deborah Sunter, also says that "a rising proportion of students are juggling full-time studies and employment." She restates the question that is bothering me: "There is

PARTICIPATION RATES IN THE LABOUR FORCE OF 15 TO 24 YEAR OLDS IN CANADA

Year	*15-19 Year Olds*	*20-24 Year Olds*
1961	36.6*	68.9
1971	42.9	72.4
1976	49.8	76.2
1981	55.7	79.7
1983	51.5	79.1
1988	57.3	80.8

Note: *14 to 19 year olds

Source: Maureen Baker, "Canadian Youth in a Changing World." Extracted from Statistics Canada, *Historical Labour Force Statistics*, Cat. 71-201, Ottawa, 1973; Statistics Canada, *Historical Labour Force Statistics – Actual Data, Seasonal Data, Seasonally Adjusted Data, 1988*, Cat. 71-201, 1988, Ottawa, January 1989, p.242.

PERCENTAGE OF FULL-TIME STUDENTS WHO ALSO HOLD JOBS, 1990 SCHOOL YEAR*

	Total	*Secondary*	*Community College*	*University*
Both Sexes	39	39	43	37
15-16 years	34	35	–	–
17-19 years	44	48	45	32
20-24 years	39	–	42	39
Men	38	39	43	33
15-16 years	34	34	–	–
17-19 years	43	46	44	27
20-24 years	36	–	42	34
Women	41	40	43	41
15-16 years	35	35	–	–
17-19 years	45	50	45	35
20-24 years	43	–	42	44

Note: *September 1990 to April 1991 averages.

Source: Deborah Sunter, "Juggling School and Work." Statistics Canada.

concern that academic achievement may be diminished by work hours that compete for study time, especially when students work long hours at jobs that have little relevance to their school programs . . . On the other hand, when school and work are successfully combined, students may gain valuable skills that better prepare them for the job market and adult life." Her study shows how many young people are working, but doesn't answer the questions: is it good, bad? helpful, harmful? "On the positive side, there is general agreement that students who work while attending school more easily find employment after leaving school. They also tend to earn more than their non-working counterparts, at least in the initial stages of post-school employment . . . Some researchers have found no demonstrable negative effects of paid work on academic achievement. Others suggest that working students tend to get lower grades and are less likely to complete their academic program or go on to higher education, especially when they work long weekly hours at jobs that are unrelated to their studies. Thus, in the long term, working students may be less able to compete in the labour market than their non-working counterparts."

Peter Dalglish, the founder of Street Kids International, puts forward another argument: "If you abolish child labour, you're ultimately just going to disenfranchise the kids you're trying to protect . . . Focussing on legislation alone is not an adequate solution. What we need even more than legal reform is economic development, political reform and direct action for social justice." Quoted in an article by Joseph Gathia from the newsletter of the International Centre for Human Rights and Democratic Development, Dalglish insists that children have the right to work *and* the right not to be exploited. Some examples of this exploitation:

- child labourers in Indonesian lightbulb factories earn three dollars a week;
- half the children in Pakistan's carpet industry die by age twelve from malnutrition and disease;
- child labourers are exposed to toxic chemicals in Indian factories for five dollars a month;

- as many as 800,000 girls between the ages of twelve and fifteen work as prostitutes in Thailand, where tourists travel for "sex tours."

If children are going to work, or if they have to work, there must be laws, enforceable laws, to make sure that they are not exploited and killed by their employers.

❖

The rest of this section includes material on international youth employment laws and children's rights, Canada's federal law on the minimum age for employment, and information from across the country about minimum working age restrictions and exemptions.

United Nations Convention on the Rights of the Child

Article 32 of the United Nations' Convention on the Rights of the Child deals with children's rights as they apply to work:

1. States Parties [States party to the Convention] recognize the right of the child to be protected from economic exploitation and from performing any work that is likely to be hazardous or to interfere with the child's education, or to be harmful to the child's health or physical, mental, spiritual, moral or social development.

2. States Parties shall take legislative, administrative, social and education measures to ensure the implementation of the present article. To this end, and having regard to the relevant provisions of other international instruments, States Parties shall in particular:

a. Provide for a minimum age or minimum ages for admissions to employment;

b. Provide for appropriate regulation of the hours and conditions of employment;

c. Provide for appropriate penalties or other sanctions to ensure the effective enforcement of the present article.

ILO Minimum Age Convention

The International Labor Organization in Geneva drafted the Minimum Age Convention (No. 138) in 1973.

Article 1

Each Member for which this Convention is in force undertakes to pursue a national policy designed to ensure the effective abolition of child labour and to raise progressively the minimum age for admission to employment or work to a level consistent with the fullest physical and mental development of young persons.

Article 2

1. Each Member which ratifies this Convention shall specify, in a declaration appended to its ratification, a minimum age for admission to employment or work within its territory and on means of transport registered in its territory: subject to Articles 4 to 8 of this Convention, no one under that age shall be admitted to employment or work in any occupation . . .

3. The minimum age specified in pursuance of paragraph 1 of this Article shall not be less than the age of completion of compulsory schooling and, in any case, shall not be less than fifteen years.

4. Notwithstanding the provisions of paragraph 3 of this Article, a Member whose economy and educational facilities are insufficiently developed may, after consultation with the organization of employers and workers concerned, where such exist, initially specify a minimum age of fourteen years . . .

Article 3

1. The minimum age for admission to any type of employment or work which by its nature or the circumstances in which it is carried out is likely to jeopardize the health, safety, or morals of young persons shall not be less than eighteen years . . .

3. Notwithstanding the provisions of paragraph 1 of this Article, national laws or regulations or the competent authority may, after consultation with the organizations of employers and workers concerned, where such exist, authorize employment or work as from the age of sixteen years on condition that the health, safety, and morals of the young persons concerned are fully protected and that the young persons have received adequate specific instruction or vocational training in the relevant branch of activity . . .

Article 5

3. The provisions of the Convention shall be applicable as a minimum to the following: mining and quarrying; manufactur-

ing; construction; electricity, gas and water; sanitary services; transport, storage and communication; and plantations and other agricultural undertakings mainly producing for commercial purposes but excluding family and small-scale holdings producing for local consumption and not regularly employing hired workers.

Article 6

This Convention does not apply to work done by children and young persons in schools for general, vocational, or technical education or in other training institutions, or to work done by persons at least 14 years of age in undertakings, where such work is carried out in accordance with conditions prescribed by the competent authority . . .

Article 7

1. National laws or regulations may permit the employment or work of persons thirteen to fifteen years of age on light work which is –

(a) not likely to be harmful to their health or development; and

(b) not such as to prejudice their attendance at school, their participation in vocational orientation or training programmes approved by the competent authority or their capacity to benefit from the instruction received.

Canada's Federal and Provincial Laws

Twelve pages of tables from Canada's labour ministry outline the different employment standards legislation that is in place throughout the country. School-leaving age is fifteen in B.C., New Brunswick, Newfoundland, Québec, and the Northwest Territories, and sixteen in the remaining provinces and the Yukon.

There is no absolute minimum age for employment in Canada. Federally, a child cannot be employed under the age of seventeen unless he or she is "not required to be at school . . . and the work involved falls outside excluded categories and is unlikely to endanger health or safety. Never between 11 p.m. and 6 a.m."

Every province has legislation which allows for children to be employed at an age younger than seventeen, but with added stipulations ranging from "with written consent of parent or guardian" to "not in employment that is or is likely to be unwholesome or harmful to the person's health, welfare or moral or physical development." There is legislation about what children *can* do (work as a delivery person, clerk, messenger, musician, actor, or shoe-shiner) and what they can't do (work in a logging outfit, underground in a mine, operating machinery, as an atomic radiation worker). Only in Saskatchewan can a person under sixteen years old become an apprentice.

Housing

In the report *Changing Course: An NDP Action Plan on Poverty*, Chris Axworthy includes the following information, from 1991 Canada Mortgage and Housing Corporation stats: 77 percent of "welfare" households with children (50 percent or more of their income came from social assistance payments) are in core housing need – but these "welfare" households make up only 33 percent of all households with children in core housing needs. This means that the remaining 67 percent of families in core housing need are "working poor."

Veronica Doyle of the Canadian Housing and Renewal Association writes in *Housing and Children in Canada*:

> The Core Housing Need Model defines households to be in "core need" (i.e. they qualify for federal housing assistance, if available) when they occupy housing that does not meet current standards for suitability (i.e. crowding), adequacy (i.e. the unit has all basic plumbing facilities and requires, at most, only minor upkeep) and affordability (i.e. shelter costs are at 30 percent or less of the household's income) and the household's income is below the income at which a household could rent a unit which is suitable and appropriate at the average market rent – the Core Need Income Threshold (CNIT) . . . CNITs are set at the income required to pay the average market rent for a fully serviced unit at a 30 percent rent-geared-to-income ratio. For example, if the average rent in a city for a two-bedroom apartment was $600, the CNIT for

a household for which a two-bedroom unit was appropriate would be $2000 per month, or $24,000 per year.

Doyle recommends that the federal government "develop a new perspective on housing for purposes of policy and program development"; specifically that it "consider the housing needs of children from a preventive health perspective. There is an established relationship between adequate, uncrowded and affordable basic shelter which is safe, secure and appropriate to children's developmental needs and a child's physical and mental health, development and future well-being." She argues that housing should be a *right*, as spelled out in the Universal Declaration of Human Rights, Article 25(1).

"The Core Need Index must be based on definitions of household which correspond to the present range of household type, rather than the one-earner/one-homemaker norm of past decades," writes Doyle. "It must take into account the locational and support requirements of households such as single-parent and aboriginal families, as well as safety, security of tenure and design appropriate for children . . . If a single parent spends more than 30 percent of income to access housing which is near necessary services and day care, it would not be considered in need if less expensive housing were available, even though its location might

NUMBER AND PERCENT OF CHILDREN AND HOUSEHOLDS WITH CHILDREN IN CORE HOUSING NEED, 1988

Tenure	*Number of Households With Children*	*Number of Children*
Owners	94,000 (29%)	182,000 (31%)
Renters	232,000 (71%)	411,000 (69%)
Total	326,000 (100%)	593,000 (100%)

Source: Veronica Doyle, *Housing and Children in Canada*, with data from Statistics Canada Household Income, Facilities and Equipment and Shelter Cost Survey micro-data tape, 1988, enhanced to facilitate calculations of core housing need made by the Research Division, Canada Mortgage and Housing Corporation.

require considerably more travel with small children each day. This family is deemed to be living where it does by choice."

Finally, Doyle recommends that the government:

- Expand and enhance the strengths of existing programs.
- Maintain a federal role in housing to sustain national standards of housing policy and programs while encouraging local priority setting, delivery and management of housing.
- Increase the supply of non-profit and cooperative housing targeted to households in core housing need.
- Strengthen the capacity of the non-profit sector to develop and maintain housing outside the for-profit market.
- Assist public and non-profit housing managers to develop more participatory management structures.
- Continue to support the search for innovative methods to expand the supply of housing available to people with moderate means.

Many young women that I have spoken to over the years have lived with a boyfriend because they didn't earn enough to pay rent on their own. Once upon a time, the common sense rule was that 25 percent of one's income should pay for shelter and the rest for support. One of the problems with homeless youth and adults is that jobs don't pay enough to rent a decent accommodation, especially since rents have climbed higher and higher. So, just as in the U.S. where working people are forced to live in shelters, working Canadians are not able to rent a place to live and put food on their tables.

Health and Nutrition

> A child who is impoverished is 2.8 times more likely to experience chronic problems with physical health and 1.7 times more likely to have chronic emotional problems.
>
> Mel Gill, executive director of the Ottawa-Carleton Children's Aid Society

Other Issues Affecting Children

❖

Although poverty does not mean that a child will necessarily have health problems, it is strongly correlated with increased risks of illness, psychological problems and death. There are many ways of explaining this link. Lack of money affects the quantity and quality of food, and an inadequate diet prevents a child from properly developing physically, mentally and emotionally. Poverty also creates anxiety and stress which may affect the mental and physical health of parents and children. Poverty may mean playing on the street, or coming home to an empty house because both parents are at work and cannot afford adequate childcare.

from *The Health of Canada's Children: A Canadian Institute of Child Health Profile*, 1989

Each stress factor in a child's life . . . magnifies the effects of every other, so the child who suffers from a multiplicity of stresses, such as overcrowding, paternal delinquency, poor schooling, or abuse, is at very high risk.

Child Poverty and Adult Social Problems, quoted from "Prevention Now," a report by the National Task Force on Preventative Strategies in Children's Mental Health, 1984

A quarter of a million of the world's young children are dying every week, and millions more are surviving in the half-life of malnutrition and almost permanent ill health.

from UNICEF's 1992 report on the state of the world's children

The infant mortality rate is 2.5 times higher for the poorest area of Toronto than for the wealthiest. For Canada as a whole, it is 1.9 times higher.

Death from birth defects is 1.5 times higher among the poor.

Death from infectious disease is 2.5 times higher.

Death from accidents is twice as common among poor children.

Death by fire, falls, drowning, and motor vehicle accidents are more than four times as common.

Low birth weight babies are twice as common among the poor as among the wealthy. Prematurity is also more common.

Poor children weigh less and are shorter.

Other conditions that have been associated with poverty include:

- Sudden infant death syndrome
- Higher suicide rates
- Obesity in girls
- Higher homicide rates
- High blood lead levels
- Increased narcotic addiction
- Iron deficiency anemia
- Increased drug & alcohol abuse
- Dental caries
- Increased antisocial behaviour
- Upper respiratory tract infection
- Increased learning disability
- Chronic ear infections
- Increased child abuse
- Mental retardation
- Decreased school performance.

Statistics gathered by Dr. Chandrakant P. Shah
of the Hospital for Sick Children in Toronto

PERCENTAGE OF POOR AND NON-POOR CHILDREN, 6-16 YEARS, WITH VARIOUS HEALTH AND RELATED PROBLEMS

	Family income status	
Characteristic	*Poor*	*Not poor*
Emotional disorder	11.2	5.2
Hyperactivity	13.2	5.3
Conduct disorder	16.9	4.8
Regular smoker	25.6	11.6
Poor school performance	29.7	13.3
Chronic health problems	30.1	17.6

Source: Senate Standing Committee, *Children in Poverty*, from Dan Offord, Mike Boyle, and Yvonne Racine, *Ontario Child Health Study: Children at Risk*, July 1989, as well as Dr. Offord's testimony given to the Standing Senate Committee on Social Affairs, Science and Technology, March 20, 1990.

A major, and life-long cost to society of raising children in poverty is that they perform poorly at school; drop out of school in greater numbers before completing high school; and end up more frequently as low-productivity and intermittently employed workers ... There are two main reasons [why this is so]: a deprived material environment leads to many unmet needs and alienation, which is detrimental to providing a proper learning environment; and poor physical and mental health resulting from being raised in poverty makes learning difficult.

The link between poverty and poor child health is well documented. In 1986, the mortality rate from all causes for children under 20 years of age in Canada was 56 percent higher among children from poor families than it was among higher income families. Infant mortality (first year of life), in the same year, was twice as high for poor as for higher income families.

Children in Poverty: Toward a Better Future

There are more food bank outlets in this country today than any single restaurant or grocery supermarket chain – even outnumbering McDonald's!

Gerard Kennedy, executive director
of the Canadian Association of Food Banks

... in spite of the fact that children make up only 26 percent of the Canadian population, they account for approximately 40 percent of the users of food banks.

Nova Scotia Nutrition Council

Who would have thought that in the 1990s we would be feeding children in food banks and soup kitchens?

Helen Saravanamuttoo of
the Child Poverty Action Group (Ottawa-Carleton)

Child Benefits

While there are various reasons – political, social and economic – why Canada established its child benefit programs over the years, the system can be viewed as having four main objectives:

a. parental recognition – to acknowledge the contribution that all parents make to society in raising future citizens, workers and taxpayers.

b. horizontal equity – to help recognize the fact that parents have heavier financial demands than childless couples and single persons with the same (pre-transfer) incomes, since the labour market does not vary wages according to family size.

c. anti-poverty – to supplement the incomes of lower-income families with children.

d. economic stimulus – to put cash into the hands of parents and thus stimulate consumer demand and the economic benefits that follow.

Ken Battle, "Child Benefits Reform,"
in *Children in Poverty*, July 1990

Until the 1980s there were five programs of benefits or tax credits/exemptions available for parents:

The Family Allowance cheque filled the objectives of parental recognition and horizontal equity, as it was sent to every child, through his or her parents. In 1973 this benefit was made taxable, in 1986 was partially de-indexed to inflation, and in 1989 a "clawback" was instituted, which meant that although the cheques were still sent out to all families, the wealthiest paid the entire benefit back at tax time.

The Child Tax Exemption was changed in 1988 to a non-refundable credit. As an exemption, this filled the objective of horizontal equity, as it was available to all families and provided the largest benefit to those in the highest tax bracket. The credit allows for vertical equity, as all families can claim the same amount of money, but this amount is less than was available through the exemption.

The Refundable Child Tax Credit is an anti-poverty measure, available to families below a certain threshold of income. It can be claimed against taxes owing or, if no taxes are owed, can be claimed as a payment from the government.

The Equivalent-to-Married Exemption/Credit can be claimed for one child if the parent is single. This credit is not refundable (i.e., you can apply it against taxes you owe, but it will not be given to you in cash if you owe no taxes), so it is of no help to non-tax-paying parents.

The Child Care Expense Deduction is available to parents who can provide childcare receipts.

All these benefits and deductions are partially de-indexed, which means that their value is eroded as inflation rises (the $2000 you get this year is worth less in buying power than the $2000 you got two years ago).

In his report "Child Benefits Reform," Ken Battle concluded:

> all the traditional objectives of child benefits are being jeopardized by the changes made over the last five years. The anti-poverty/income supplementation role of child benefits will weaken steadily over time, unless something is done to stem their erosion from inflation. The goal of horizontal equity has been severely compromised, leaving many higher-income families with a token and dwindling benefit. To the extent that child benefits help stimulate consumer demand – the available evidence indicates that their economic impact is probably fairly small – it can be argued that their erosion will further reduce this effect as well.
>
> The savings that are being realized through the partial de-indexation of child benefits are massive albeit hidden from public view. We estimate that more than $3.5 billion will be removed from the child benefits system between 1986 and 1991. These savings are being applied to deficit reduction and are not being redistributed to low-income families.
>
> The recent child benefits reforms have not traded off the goal of horizontal equity in favour of strengthening the anti-poverty goal. Rather, they have siphoned off resources from the child benefits system to meet another objective of public policy that has

overshadowed social policy purposes in recent years – deficit reduction.

In February 1992, partly as a response to the Senate Sub-Committee on Poverty, the Conservative government announced in its budget a new monthly child benefit replacing the refundable and non-refundable child tax credits and family allowances. Also announced was an earned-income supplement of up to $500 for low-income working families (with earnings between $3750 and $25,921).

The new benefit is

- the same as the maximum amount that was provided by family allowance and the refundable child tax credit;
- aimed at low and middle-income families (families receive lesser amounts as their income rises above $25,921 a year; benefits disappear when family income reaches $70,981 a year);
- partially de-indexed;
- increased by $213 a year for each child under age seven for whom a family does not claim the Child Care Expense Deduction;
- increased by $75 for the third child in a family and for every child after the third.

The Equivalent-to-Married Credit was still available to single-parent families, and the Child Care Expense Deduction was increased. The day after the budget speech, the government announced that it would not be implementing a government-supported system of childcare.

In its report, *The 1992 Budget and Child Benefits*, the National Council of Welfare concludes that "one of the striking features of the proposed new child tax benefit is that the vast majority of families would be better off under the new system than they are under the current system." However, "a disproportionate number of single-parent mothers rely on welfare as their main source of income, and none of these families would get any increases in benefits under the White Paper proposals . . . A single-parent family with no earned income would receive $1,233 from the child tax benefit . . . At the other extreme, a [single-parent] family with earnings of $100,000 would get no child benefit but a total of $1,418 in tax savings from the Equivalent-to-Married Credit." And a "family with no earnings would get $2,253 a year in benefits and [a] family earning $100,000 would get $2,240" when savings from the Child Care Expense Deduction are factored in.

Linda Marcotte, writing End Legislated Poverty's reaction to the budget, wrote that "the end of universality of the family allowance is very significant. With middle and higher income people not benefitting from the program, their support for it will erode or end. This will undermine political support for the meagre benefits that low-income people do get, and make us vulnerable to more cutbacks."

Both the National Council of Welfare and End Legislated Poverty, among other groups, protested the fact that the earned-income supplement was only available to parents who were working. Families earning less than $21,000 were to receive up to $500 a year under the program. That amount would decrease for families earning between $21,000 and $26,000, and at $26,000 a family would receive no earned-income supplement. The NCW argued, "Child benefits are paid by the federal government to parents, but they are really intended for children. We believe that children should be entitled to benefits on the basis of family income alone. They should not have their benefits raised or lowered simply because their parents happen to be in or out of the paid labour force at some point in their lives." Linda Marcotte of ELP questioned the government's aims, asking, "Was this change put into place so government wouldn't have to raise minimum wages or give women pay equity?"

The NCW also urged that the benefit be fully indexed to inflation, that the Child Care Expense Deduction be changed to a tax credit, and that the federal government ensure that provincial governments did not cut their benefits because of the new federal system.

The following articles present views from anti-poverty workers on the new child benefit system.

Bill C-80

The following is an excerpt from the National Anti-Poverty Organization's (NAPO) written submission to the legislative committee of the House of Commons studying Bill C-80, the legislation to enact the child tax benefit. The bill was introduced in Parliament on May 13, 1992, given Royal Assent on October 15, 1992, and came into effect on January 1, 1993.

❖

Among NAPO's founding principles was the right of poor Canadians to participate in discussions on policies and programs that affect them. Family allowances, the child tax credit, and the refundable child tax credit are programs that certainly affected the well-being of poor Canadian families. Any changes to these programs is of great interest to NAPO.

The old system was far from perfect, but it helped poor families.

NAPO sees family allowances as a recognition by the federal government of the invaluable work contributed by parents (and particularly mothers, who were the usual recipients of FA) to the well-being of all Canadians through their taking on the primary responsibility for the caring of the country's children. An added advantage of the family allowance program is that it is universal. To poor parents, this means that it is non-stigmatizing. There are no demeaning means tests to pass in order to get your monthly cheque. There is no decrease or cut-off of benefits at arbitrary income levels. Bill C-80 proposes to eliminate family allowances. This means that the federal government will no longer recognize the unique contribution of parents to the development of Canada.

The refundable child tax credit is a way for the federal government to redistribute income from richer Canadians to poorer Canadian parents. It recognizes the importance of providing every parent with the means to take care of children in an optimal way and attempts to alleviate the disadvantages of poverty. The refundable child tax credit could be better: it could be richer, fully indexed, with higher thresholds. Nonetheless, this targeted subsidy serves a useful purpose in Canada's income redistribution system.

The child credit is very small, yet useful to any family with taxes owing.

The federal government says that the new system will be a bigger help to poor families because it will be targeted.

The federal government says that its new integrated child tax benefit will be a bigger help to poor families because it will be better targeted. Family allowances will no longer go to every family, but only to those who need the money, they say. The money thus freed up – as well as an extra $400 million a year that the federal government will contribute – will be better targeted, they say.

NAPO says that the new benefit is no more targeted than the old system.

What Bill C-80 does is make clear what the federal government was already doing to family allowances. Family allowances were no longer universal because of the "clawback" provision. Individuals with incomes over $50,000 saw their family allowances taxed back. In effect, family allowances were no longer available to them. The new system will not change anything for them. NAPO rejects the government's argument that the new system provides for more effective targeting of benefits.

For families where more than one parent works and the combined parents' income is over $50,000, the new child benefit package will be lower than the old package because the threshold above which benefits start diminishing is now based on combined family income. The federal government calls this better targeting. NAPO calls it a disincentive for families to try getting out of poverty through both parents participating in the labour force.

The federal government says that the new system will be fairer. NAPO says that the new system creates two classes of poor, and discriminates against the poorest.

NAPO objects strongly to the "earned-income supplement" in the new child benefit package. This supplement in effect destroys all the advantages of the new package because it completely negates any benefit to the poorest of the poor – those living on incomes derived from the grossly inadequate social assistance programs of the different provinces and territories.

Working poor parents definitely need financial help in raising their children. They cannot be expected to provide nutritious food, safe housing, and opportunities for developmental growth on incomes that are below the poverty line. However, a maximum supplement of $500 will provide little help.

Working poor families need affordable childcare for their children. They need housing options that are affordable and appropriate to their families' needs. They need jobs paying decent wages and providing adequate benefits. Yet, in previous budgets, the federal government has slashed funding for non-profit housing. It has concentrated on the goals of deficit reduction and the fight against inflation at the expense of job creation.

Recently, the federal government has announced that it cannot afford to contribute to the creation of childcare spaces. Instead, it has chosen to increase the Child Care Expense Deduction for families with receipted childcare. It has taken this decision knowing full well that tax deductions benefit richer families more than poorer families. It also knows that poorer families are more likely not to have childcare receipts and thus cannot claim the tax deduction.

If the government had wanted to truly help working poor families, it could have chosen to do many things – or even to rescind some of its recent budget decisions. Instead, it chose to create a very small "earned-income supplement" that creates two classes of poor families – those who are working and those on welfare.

Poor people are continually fighting against stereotypes created by people who have never experienced poverty and who are full of judgments. One of these stereotypes is the difference between the "deserving" and the "undeserving" poor. These labels are used to discriminate among different types of poverty. "Deserving" poor are worthy of society's help/charity while "undeserving" poor are not.

Bill C-80 in effect says that the federal government has decided that working poor families are part of the "deserving" poor and has decreed that they would be helped with a maximum amount of $500 a year. This, the government says, would reinforce the incentives for poor parents to participate in the work force.

By the same token, Bill C-80 says that families on social assistance – those with an earned income below $3,750 a year – are "undeserving" of further federal government assistance because they are not working. This completely ignores many facts over which poor parents have very little control:

- Jobs offering decent wages and benefits are very hard to find, especially if one is a single parent with sole responsibility of children and few opportunities for skills upgrading.
- Full-time jobs available to those with limited skills are disappearing.
- The minimum wage is not keeping up with inflation so that jobs paying wages at, or close to, the minimum wage are no longer a guarantee of incomes above the poverty line.
- Regulated childcare options are dwindling and increasingly expensive. Unless government-subsidized, they are far beyond the reach of poor parents.
- Social assistance rates are much lower than the poverty line; if the government is trying to have an impact on child poverty, to completely ignore families living on social assistance makes no sense.

In effect, Bill C-80 does not change the amount of money received by two types of families:

- those with yearly incomes over $50,000 to $75,000 (the increased Child Care Expense Deduction will more than compensate these families);
- those with yearly incomes under $3,750 (that is, the poorest of the poor).

We say: by all means, provide more benefits to working poor families! But do it in a way that makes a difference. And don't freeze out welfare families! To do so is hypocritical and discriminatory.

The federal government says that the new benefits are more generous. NAPO asks: What is your definition of generous?

The federal government proudly announces that it will add a yearly amount of $400 million to the child benefits package, and that this new money makes the new child benefits package more generous. This begs the question: more generous for whom?

It isn't generous for welfare families.

It is true that some families will receive more under the new plan. But we repeat: the new package does not provide one extra penny to welfare families. Yet welfare rates do not even provide these families with enough money to buy enough food to feed their children until the end of each month, let alone money for clothing, recreational activities, and extra expenses incurred in our "free" educational system.

It isn't generous for working poor families either.

The new package will not provide enough money to working poor families and families living on modest incomes to make a difference. The "earned-income supplement" is meant to be a work incentive for those on social assistance. In reality, it is a poor substitute to a policy of full employment at decent wages and a federally supported childcare program.

It isn't generous when it is compared to the accumulated cuts to child-related benefits.

The extra $400 million is little when compared to the $3.5 billion siphoned from child benefits since 1985 when partial de-indexing of benefits was first introduced. And it is worth noting that this new "generous" package is still partially de-indexed, thus insuring that it will be of lesser and lesser use to families through the years.

It isn't generous when it is compared to the accumulated cuts to social spending in previous federal budgets.

The extra money is also little when compared to other federal budget cuts: cuts to social housing, a freeze on Canada Assistance Plan contributions for three provinces, cuts to the Canadian Jobs Strategy, cuts to the federal contributions under Established Programs Financing. All these cuts have a very real and direct impact on poor families in Canada.

Although the new child benefits package does contain more federal money, it is very little compared to the combined year-over-year budget cuts to other programs affecting Canadian families. This is why NAPO asks what definition the federal government is using to describe the new package as generous.

NAPO wants to know how the new child benefit will be treated by the provincial and territorial welfare offices.

NAPO is concerned with the treatment of the new child benefit by the provincial and territorial welfare offices. Because it will be a benefit delivered monthly, it will be at greater risk of being taken into account in (or deducted from) monthly welfare cheques.

This is not a frivolous concern. In the province of Saskatchewan, it is the practice to deduct family allowances from welfare cheques. The province has claimed that welfare rates were adjusted up to compensate for this deduction. However, since welfare rates in Saskatchewan are far from among the highest in Canada, it is difficult to see that the adjustment was meaningful.

Welfare rights groups in Saskatchewan are now worried that the full amount of the new benefit will be deducted from welfare cheques. This would meant that they would have lost not only their family allowances but also their refundable child tax credit.

NAPO opposes the proposed new child benefit because it will do nothing to help alleviate child poverty.

When the federal government started talking about a new child benefits package, it talked about a new child benefit that would help alleviate child poverty. NAPO shares the government's concern about child poverty. However, we want to see a real plan to alleviate child poverty, one that will make a real difference.

As long as there are poor families, there will be poor children. The key element to alleviating child poverty is to eradicate poverty in general. And the way to do this is to put in place an income redistribution system that sees benefits flowing from the rich to the poor.

The proposed child benefit does not do this. Instead . . .

- It discriminates against a category of poor families – welfare families.
- Although it provides for an extra $400 million a year, it is proposed at the same time as the increased Child Care Expense Deduction for families with receipted childcare expenses (the vast majority of whom will not be poor).

- It is too little too late. It comes after seven years of partial de-indexation of income tax credits, after three consecutive years of cuts in federal contributions to social housing, the Canada Assistance Plan and Established Programs Financing, and many more budget measures that made life that much more difficult for Canadian families generally and poor families specifically.

We therefore ask your committee to recommend rejection of Bill C-80.

Tory Government Sneaks in the Big Business Version of the Guaranteed Annual Income

This article by Jean Swanson of End Legislated Poverty appeared in the NAPO newsletter during the summer of 1992.

The latest budget of the federal Conservative government seems to be another step in the direction of a Big Business version of a Guaranteed Annual Income (GAI). The following is my analysis of how the Tories are gradually sneaking in what is really a form of guaranteed poverty.

For years, poor people have wanted a GAI that would provide at least a poverty-level income for all. In its 1986 brief to the MacDonald Commission on the Economy, the Canadian Manufacturer's Association (CMA) proposed the Big Business version of the GAI. MacDonald virtually adopted the CMA's GAI proposal for the final report of his Royal Commission.

This version of the GAI, which would guarantee continued and increasing poverty for both poor-and middle-income people, has four parts:

1. Keep the amount of the GAI low. The MacDonald Commission recommended a figure that was about one-third of the poverty level – less than the present amount of welfare.

2. Destroy existing social programs. Among other programs, the CMA and MacDonald proposed ending family allowance, child tax credits, federal contributions to provinces for welfare, social housing and even the Guaranteed Income Supplement for seniors.

3. Keep wages low. Minimum wages should be kept low and pay equity laws should stay as they are, according to the MacDonald Commission.

4. Use the GAI as a wage top-up so that employers won't have to pay cost-of-living wages to their workers.

Let us look at what has happened to each of these four parts of the Big Business versions of the GAI in the 1992 federal budget.

In the budget, the Tories announced their intention to combine family allowances and child tax credits into a monthly payment for some families. They called this the Child Benefit, not a GAI.

Now, let's see if the child benefit fits the four parts of the Big Business version of the GAI.

1. Keep the income low. The amount of the child benefit is exactly the same as the combined total of the old family allowance and child tax credits – $1,020 per one-child family.

2. Destroy existing social programs. The child benefit results in the destruction of existing social programs, the family allowance and the child tax credits. Along with the child benefit, the government announced that it would also destroy the co-operative housing program (for newly established co-ops), which is a social program that benefits low- and middle-income families.

3. Keep wages low. The federal government has not raised the minimum wage since 1986. At $4.00 per hour, it is lower than the minimum wage in any province. In addition, both the provincial and the federal governments have frozen minimum wages for long periods. For example, in British Columbia, the Social Credit government froze the minimum wage for six years at $3.65, while inflation ravaged the purchasing power of Canadians . . . The federal budget also announced that the government will not pay the retroactive pay equity claims of about $1 billion to approximately 70,000 workers, most of whom are women employed in the public sector.

4. Allow the GAI to be used as a wage top-up for inadequate wages. In February 1991, when Linda Marcotte made a presentation to the Parliamentary Committee on Child Poverty on behalf of End

Legislated Poverty (ELP), she described ELP's position on the child benefit. Marcotte asked Committee Chairperson Barbara Greene if the benefit was to be used for the child only or for the family. Greene responded that "the minimum wage would not have to cover the costs of raising children, just the adult."

Because of the long-term minimum wage freeze, the British Columbia minimum wage would now have to be about $8.26 per hour to be at the same percent of the poverty line that it was in 1975.

Clearly, the Tories don't want minimum wages to increase. Instead, they want the child benefit to act as a wage supplement for employers who refuse to pay a cost-of-living wage.

In the last budget, the government also put into its child benefit a grant of up to $500 for low-income working families.

The Tories have not called their child benefit a GAI. But government officials have noted that when the child benefit system is in place, they will also have in place an administrative system for delivering their version of the GAI.

Some of the dangers of this Big Business version of the GAI: the amount is too low; existing social programs, which are much-needed, are destroyed; and the decent wages necessary for poor people to escape poverty are omitted.

Some of the more hidden dangers, however, are:

- *Canada Assistance Plan (CAP)*: Through CAP, the federal government pays nearly half of provincial social services and welfare costs. Because it says welfare is a right, CAP provides an appeal system for people who have been denied all or part of the welfare to which they believe themselves to be entitled. If welfare is administered through the tax system, which includes no legal rights for poor people, poor people could be in an even worse position than we are now.
- *Unfairness*: The Goods and Services Tax (GST) transferred $4 billion in taxes from the corporate sector to individuals, most of whom are already hard-pressed.

  The Big Business version of the GAI would transfer wage payments, not tax payments, from the corporate sector to middle-and lower-income earners.

My analysis is that this process allows corporations to exploit people living on welfare, using them as cheap labour.

- *The end of universal programs*: Universal programs, such as family allowances, have helped to create equity among all citizens. Studies have shown that programs targeting poor people are poor programs. Furthermore, middle-income people may no longer support programs that do not benefit them – a phenomenon which will erode general political support for such programs.
- *Poverty will be increased*: The Big Business version of the GAI will increase poverty, not end it. A tax credit, which is a supplement to earnings, is not as positive as it may seem. The government will still continue with its low-wage strategy, keeping minimum wages low, denying pay equity, and, through high unemployment, keeping the competition for jobs high. In addition, families lose the child tax credit, family allowance, and the chance for a unit in co-operative housing.

  Senior citizens may lose the Guaranteed Income Supplement, which is the only program that brings their income closer to the poverty line than that of any other low-income group.

In conclusion, to end poverty, we must build a social movement to demand: decent jobs and decent wages; good insurance programs, such as unemployment insurance, Canada Pension Plan, and disability insurance; improved universal programs, such as medicare, education, and childcare; affordable housing; taxes which are based on the ability to pay; good public pensions; and responsible government that can manage and regulate our economy so that it benefits all. Finally, we need adequate income – at least to the poverty line – for people who are not completely covered by these programs.

The Bottom Line

> This study will not be to the liking of everyone interested in alleviating child poverty. By appealing to the economic self-interest of Canadians it has a restricted focus. It gives the appearance that the economic consequences of child poverty for the nation are the only important concern. However, this is not the intention of the authors or of the Senate committee . . . In developing this special study it was felt that more attention should be paid to the "bottom line" concern of what child poverty, and its association with school failure, can mean to the Canadian economy, especially as the population ages.
>
> *Children in Poverty*

ESTIMATES OF INDIVIDUAL LIFETIME INCOME SECURITY BENEFITS RECEIVED BETWEEN THE AGES OF 25 AND 65 YEARS, BY EDUCATION LEVEL AND SEX, IN 1990 $

	Education		
	0-8 years	*12 years*	*Degree*
Male			
Social assistance	$47,000	$19,000	$15,000
UI benefits	$60,000	$30,000	$14,000
Female			
Social assistance	$41,000	$13,000	$12,000
UI benefits	$21,000	$21,000	$20,000

Source: Children in Poverty, pg. 68. Tabulations based on Statistics Canada's Social Policy Simulation Database/Model, SPSD/M, which is based on the Survey of Consumer Finances micro-data tape for 1986, the Family Expenditure Survey for 1986 and Revenue Canada Taxation Statistics for 1986. Survey values have been adjusted for under-reporting and are presented in 1990 dollars. Tax burdens are estimated based on the income tax and consumption tax systems in place in 1990.

ESTIMATED ECONOMIC GAINS RESULTING FROM THE ELIMINATION OF POVERTY-INDUCED DROPPING OUT, COVERING THE PERIOD 1990-2010, BY SEX, 1990 DOLLARS

	Lifetime individual		*Lifetime total*		*Lifetime total*
Years of	*Male*	*Female*	*Male*	*Female*	*Combined*
Employment	0.9	1.8	$88,000	$172,000	$260,000
Unemployment	-0.6	-0.2	-$56,000	-$17,000	-$73,000
Out of labour force	-0.3	-1.6	-$32,000	-$155,000	-$187,000

See Source note on previous page.

ESTIMATES OF INDIVIDUAL LIFETIME TAX AND PREMIUM CONTRIBUTIONS BETWEEN THE AGES OF 25 AND 65, BY EDUCATION LEVEL AND SEX, 1990 DOLLARS

	Education		
	0-8 years	*12 years*	*Degree*
Male	*$*	*$*	*$*
Fed. income tax	$133,000	$220,000	$447,000
Fed. consumption tax	$56,000	$66,000	$93,000
Prov. income tax	$92,000	$134,000	$281,000
Prov. consumption tax	$56,000	$64,000	$91,000
UI contribution	$14,000	$19,000	$22,000
Female	*$*	*$*	*$*
Fed. income tax	$26,000	$72,000	$195,000
Fed. consumption tax	$20,000	$28,000	$48,000
Prov. income tax	$18,000	$45,000	$134,000
Prov. consumption tax	$19,000	$28,000	$48,000
UI contribution	$4,000	$10,000	$17,000

See Source note on previous page.

> Using current Statistics Canada information, research . . . projects that over the next twenty years, approximately 187,000 students will leave school due to poverty . . . These high dropout rates will cost Canadians an estimated $620 million in Unemployment Insurance costs and an additional $710 million in social assistance payments. If these high dropout rates were eliminated, research estimates that federal and provincial income taxes would rise by $7.2 billion and consumption taxes by $1.15 billion. Finally, research indicates that incomes would be $23 billion higher if poverty-induced dropouts had gone on to complete an average level of education.
>
> *Children in Poverty*

❖

In 1985, each elderly person was supported by five active labour force participants; by 2026, the ratio will be a little over two to one according to statistics in *Child Poverty and Adult Social Problems. Children in Poverty* says that, in the year 2031, there will be one elderly person for only a fraction (0.84) of a future worker

INTERNATIONAL POVERTY RATES, SELECTED HOUSEHOLDS, HEAD OF HOUSEHOLD 20-55 YEARS OF AGE

Country/Year	*All households*	*Households with children*	*Lone-parent households*
Average	11.1	12.4	24.4
Canada (1987)	13.9	15.7	45.4
France (1984)	9.9	10.4	15.8
W. Germany (1984)	6.8	7.9	25.5
Sweden (1987)	8.6	5.1	5.5
Netherlands (1987)	7.6	7.3	7.5
U.S. (1986)	18.1	23.7	53.3
U.K. (1986)	12.5	16.8	18.0

Note: Definition of poverty has been standardized across countries and represents 50 percent of median disposable household income (disposable income is post-tax, and includes transfers).

Source: Centre for International Statistics, *Economic and Social Welfare for Families and Children.*

(aged zero to nineteen), compared to 2.7 young people for every senior just a few years ago, in 1986.

❖

For those who believe people are poor because they do not want to work, which I hear quoted often in the communities, over 50 percent of heads of households of poor families worked in 1989 and half of those had full year, full-time jobs but still lived in poverty . . . The truth of the matter is that there are not enough jobs available. The government has bought the line that 8 percent unemployment is acceptable . . . 8 percent is not acceptable to anyone and particularly not to the poor and the unemployed. That policy condemns people to either cyclical bouts of poverty or a lifetime of poverty.

Shirley Carr, president of
the Canadian Labour Congress, speaking to
the House of Commons Sub-Committee on Poverty

❖

The general rate of poverty among Canadians decreased marginally from 15.1 percent to 14.9 percent between 1980 and 1986 while the rate of poverty among Canadian children increased from 15 percent to 17.6 percent over the same time period. It seems clear that in deciding to have children, people must also be consenting to increasing their risk of living in poverty; tragically it appears that having children is a liability in Canada. Solutions must be found to reverse the situation: Children must be seen as our future, and as such, we must invest in them.

Changing Course: An NDP Action Plan on Poverty

❖

In a column in the Vancouver *Sun* of March 5, 1993, Ken MacQueen writes about "Crime Prevention in Canada," a report by the justice committee of the House of Commons. McQueen says the committee members' conclusion was: "it is easier, nicer, and more cost effective to offer better day care, social services, literacy programs, and counselling for young people than to foot the $51,000 annual cost of graduation to federal prison." He refers to a Michigan study that showed that every dollar invested in pre-school programs offered to three- and four-year-old children from "deprived families" saved five dollars "down the road."

❖

> It's impossible to make ends meet on welfare. How can anyone stretch $200 after rent to buy diapers and formula and baby clothes and groceries, just basic necessities? Ask any of the mothers on the street. They'll tell you that welfare forces us out here to sell our bodies to feed our kids. If welfare was tied to the real cost of living, or if we were allowed to work for extra money, some of us could make it. But if we earn legal, they deduct it from our cheques, so we're screwed either way. Hidden work is the only way out. For girls without good educations that means shit work at shit wages – women's work, right? – or hooking, which is shit work for good wages if you don't have to give money to a man.
>
> quoted by Marlene Webber in
> *Street Kids: The Tragedy of Canada's Runaways*

❖

Mildred Kerr of Equal Justice for All, an anti-poverty group in Saskatchewan, has said, "For one person to live at the poverty line in Saskatoon, she needs $900 a month. Minimum wage will bring in $800 gross before deductions." Jennifer Hyndman of the Social Planning Council of Edmonton painted the picture in more graphic terms: "a single mother with two children . . . earning the minimum wage . . . would have to work 91 hours a week in paid work to earn the StatsCan low income cut-off" Trevor Williams of Family Service Canada adds, "There is the exhaustion experienced by the lone parent caring for the child. You heard earlier about the 91 hours of work that is required just to keep a family above that line. That is 91 hours of work. Then you have to come home and look after the family as well. There are 168 hours in a week, by the way"

Minimum-wage jobs are not the answer to poverty. Jobs that pay a living wage are!

Solutions

The industry that surrounds child poverty and child abuse is a real meat market. The massive amounts of money given to studies, conferences, research, therapists, counsellors, teachers, papers, books, etc. mounts into the millions of dollars nationally. People are making a good living off the fact that we as a nation are more inclined to study than to act.

The following analogy goes through my mind. A child is stuck in quicksand, sinking an inch a day. Hundreds of people have meetings, committees are formed, money is given. One group studies the methodology of getting him out, another how he will feel after they get him out. Professionals from all over the world are flown in at great expense to ponder the situation. Translators are brought in for foreign experts and reporters. The media gets overtime as the cameras roll on the sinking child. Elizabeth Taylor, bosom heaving, offers to give her diamond to the person who can find a way to rid the world of quicksand. The Catholic church telegrams the Pope.

Unfortunately, if the child is rescued too soon, all these people will lose their status and their money flow.

The child's mother says, "Bring me a rope. I'll save my child. A strong rope. One that won't break. Something that we can depend on. I know what we need." But no one listens and the child sinks further into the quicksand and the mother has a nervous breakdown. They hospitalize her.

When the child is up to his neck in sand, almost suffocating, a SWAT team rescues him with guns drawn. I don't know why, they just always have their guns drawn. The child is then placed in a group home because his mother has given up the fight against poverty and bureaucracy and is now quietly insane.

The industry continues to employ people looking for solutions that are never implemented, and even I, in writing this book, am part of the industry, telling you about the problem, telling you what to do about it, and hoping that you will do something. This book shouldn't be needed, because there have been so many books and studies already written, and so many people working on and speaking out about this problem, but here it is. The most important thing is the children speak for themselves in this book.

❖

There are many solutions sprinkled through the pages of this book. Everyone I interviewed, children, teenagers, adults who had lived below the poverty line as children, social workers, teachers, government workers . . . all had ideas about what could be done to stop poverty, improve living conditions, deal with the problems that arose.

I've written a lot about changes that should be made in the educational system. We should educate children about poverty so they don't blame and tease their classmates, and sensitize teachers so they're more aware of students who are poor (see my "Grandma Baxter Stories" in the appendix for my idea of how we can start this education for young children). Equity of input for students and for schools is important, and there is a desperate need for quality, accessible daycare. A lot of people talked about the problem of sexual abuse – about the lack of counselling available for children (poor or otherwise) who have been abused, and about society's view of children who have been forced into prostitution. There must be prosecution and conviction of the johns! There must also be stricter screening of people who work with children, so pedophiles are not put in a position where they can abuse children.

It saves money to help a child right away rather than leaving him or her in pain once they have disclosed abuse. The longer they wait, the longer therapy will take. If they wait too long, the child will run away, and then there will be the expense of rehabilitation and group homes. Money spent now would save a child and save thousands and thousands of dollars needed later. If you arrest abusers fast, then they might be stopped. If you do nothing, then they are still sick and abusing more children who will also need therapy. Let's get with it. Prevention is where it's at, not cutbacks.

We have Big Sisters, Big Brothers – how about a program of Aunts and Uncles to help parents out with house work or a lift to buy groceries, someone for a parent to share the stress of parenting with.

Read through some of the reports listed in the bibliography. I know I've said that there are too many reports and studies and not enough being done, but these will give you an idea of where we're at, what's been done, what's been suggested. You may not agree with all of it, but in disagreement you may come up with your own solutions.

Join anti-poverty groups and groups working for children's rights and welfare (I've listed some from each province in the appendix. It's not an exhaustive list, but agencies in the main cities of each province may be able to put you in contact with groups in your particular town or city.)

Talk to your MLA, MP, and other politicians. Make sure they follow through on their promises for more jobs and a living wage (not $5.50 minimum wage!), for adequate, accessible medicare and education and social assistance, for universal childcare.

Get angry. It's easy to feel sad when you see children living on the street, panhandling, or selling themselves for sex, but sadness too often leads to feelings of hopelessness. Get angry and get active.

I was able to interview people in a variety of agencies and schools who worked with children and young people in Vancouver. I wasn't able to talk to workers with groups and agencies outside the Lower Mainland, but have read or heard about people doing things in other parts of Canada. Following are brief sketches of some other solutions and programs for children.

❖

Head & Hands is "an independent community centre based in Nôtre Dame de Grâce [Montreal] that has been helping youth for more than 20 years, providing legal, medical, educational, counselling and other services." The October 19, 1992, Montreal *Gazette* had an article about Kathleen Leahy, one of the approximately thirty street workers in the city. "I want to prevent someone from a problem down the road," she says. "For me, street work is a profession. It's a long process and there is no immediate payoff . . . I can be a resource – I go through my lists and I can lend an ear and I can bring you somewhere . . . [The reward lies in knowing] that somebody needed something and got it and they know now that they can go for help, and that they do deserve to ask for help."

❖

Alex Taylor Community School is in "one of Edmonton's toughest inner-city neighborhoods." When Steve Ramsankar took over as principal in September 1970, "kids were coming to school without breakfast. Vandalism and graffiti painted a depressing scene . . . Now it's known as a loving place'." Ramsankar worked to produce individualized language arts and math programs, an English as a Second Language program for his students' parents, a baby-sitting service for their younger brothers and sisters, and a seniors' drop-in program; daily snacks and used clothing are also available, and Christmas and New Year's Day dinners are served to members of the community. "I think we have to take care of basic physical needs in order that effective learning will take place," says Ramsankar, adding, "We have given ownership to the parents and the community, so they look out for the school." The school's Teacher-Friendly Program matches each staff member with about twelve kids: "We become their confidants and we find out more about their homes so we are able to understand why children behave in the ways they do." The result is a school where people do feel at home, and where students have a better chance of learning. (From "A nightmare is erased by a loving place," in *Education Leader*, November 6, 1992.)

❖

Campaign 2000, the national coalition of groups working to raise awareness of and to end child poverty in Canada, produced a booklet called *Fighting Poverty Through Programs*, which recommends that effective programs: be community-driven; recognize the importance of family environment and community factors; coordinate with other services; be flexible; show cultural sensitivity; emphasize prevention; provide family support, comprehensive services, transitional support, practical assistance, and personal growth/empowerment. They should work for social change, undertake research/evaluation, and be run by high-calibre, valued and respected staff.

Eight community services were listed as examples of social and health programs: the North End Parent Resource Centre in Halifax; the Montreal Diet Dispensary in Montreal; Jessie's Centre for Teenagers in Toronto; Ma Mawi Wi Chi Itata Centre in Winnipeg; Boyle-McCauley Health Centre in Edmonton; Exit Community Outreach and Wood's Homes in Calgary; Big Country Outreach Program in Drumheller; Crabtree Corner in Vancouver.

In *Dead End: Homeless Teenagers – A Multi-Service Approach,* Ray Edney writes: "Street youth run away from home in an effort to take control over lives which they have found untenable and unchangeable. They arrive on the streets with an understanding that there is no one who can help them and they are their own best caretakers. By this stage, they trust no one, and their independence is of primary importance. Attempts to restrict and restrain them, and to ignore their needs and issues are futile, because this is precisely what they have run away from." The book goes on to list three Canadian programs which have had some success in helping runaway teenagers. These are:

- DEYAS in Vancouver (see John Turvey's interview on page 152)
- Avenue 15 in Calgary, which is a shelter that provides a safe environment where teens can stay as long as they need to to get to a safer, more permanent place. They are provided with three meals a day, and advice on lifestyle skills, with an aim to getting them back with their family or set up on their own for independent living.
- S.O.S. in Toronto runs a 24-hour emergency phone, a drop-in office where teens can come to talk, use a phone to track down jobs and accommodation, and pick up food and clothing. There are four street workers doing outreach work, and there

is also a high support program in which a teen will have a personal worker, available for help and counselling fifteen hours a week.

Dead End also describes two programs in the United States. Orion Street Youth Theatre Project in Seattle, Wash., provides sixteen weeks of employment in the theatre, with morning courses in life skills and academic subjects, and afternoon work on producing and acting in a play. In Boston, The Bridge is similar to S.O.S., with outreach, counselling, food, education, and a supervised residential program.

❖

A brochure on the National Youth in Care Network describes the NYICN as an organization that allows youth to empower themselves. It says:

> In November of 1985, seven young people from across Canada were invited to attend the International Child and Youth Care Workers Conference to discuss the concept of youth empowerment. Through their participation and discussions, all seven of these young people discovered that they had one thing in common – a strong feeling of having no control over their own lives. They did not feel empowered.
>
> On an individual level, these young people felt that no one, including their social workers who were supposed to advocate on their behalf, listened to what they had to say, or asked their opinion about their case plan; a plan that has an enormous consequences for their lives. The result was a feeling of helplessness and dependency.
>
> On a broader level, these young people believe that a child welfare system that does not consult with the people it is intended to serve, will be filled with ineffective policies and attitudes that breed dependency, and relegate young people to the ranks of the homeless, friendless, jobless, and drug addicted.
>
> These seven young people had a vision – to make the child welfare system more sensitive to, and understanding of, the young people it is intended to serve. Through a process of encouraging youth to speak out and be heard, it was hoped that these young

people would have an opportunity to form friendships with those who had shared similar experiences. Their vision was to build national and local networks of youth in and from care.

When this vision was put to a group of young people at a national meeting, it was met with overwhelming support and the National Youth in Care Network was formed [in 1986].

The objectives of the NYICN are:

a) to increase awareness of the needs of youth in and from state care by researching the issues and presenting the results to youth, professionals and the general public through publications and speaking engagements, etc.

b) to provide emotional support to youth in or from state care and to guide the development of youth in care networks.

Our voting membership is comprised of young people, aged fourteen to twenty-four, who are, or have been, in the care of child welfare authorities. This membership category also includes young people who are in, or have been through, the Children's Mental Health or Young Offenders system. Non-voting members are usually comprised of adults and agencies interested, both professionally and personally, in child welfare issues.

The book *Thursday's Child*, put out by the NYICN, contains a long list of conclusions and recommendations.

I included an interview with Maggie Duckett of Gordon House Youth Works earlier in the book, but here is a description of the fourteen-week program.

For the first seven weeks, the young people take a comprehensive range of classes in life skills and employment preparation. The life skills classes cover such things as goal setting, personal ethics, self esteem, effective communication, assertiveness, problem solving, anger management/conflict resolution. Employment preparation includes topics like the pros and cons of street life, budgeting and nutrition, resumés and job applications, appearances, positive working attitudes, confidence building, and dealing with criticism. About three hours is spent on each topic.

During the eighth week of the program, participants prepare

for their off-site work experience placements. At this time their placements are confirmed and classes are specifically focused on orientation and preparation for work experience. For the next four weeks they will work at their individual jobs. There is frequent contact with, and support from, the Gordon House Youth Works staff.

Some participants move immediately into full-time employment. In other cases, the work-experience employer is not able to hire a new employee. These people return to the program for work experience feedback, supportive counselling, job search exercises, and placement assistance. Graduates of the program who are unsuccessful in finding employment are provided with continued support and assistance by Youth Works Counsellors.

Downtown South – A Gathering Place

In late 1991, Vancouver city council agreed that the city should look into providing services – including a safe house of some sort – to residents in the Downtown South area, around Granville Street. Diane MacKenzie, manager of the Carnegie Centre, was asked to find out what Downtown South residents thought about the idea of a community centre of some kind. The following are excerpts from her report to city council in July 1992.

❖

The City employee assigned to this task had no previous knowledge of the Downtown South area. Consequently, she has tried to learn about the community by seeing it through the eyes of others.

Over the first months of this year she travelled the streets in the company of hotel residents, street kids, service providers, real estate agents, merchants, architects, city staff, police and politicians. These tour guides were very generous with their knowledge.

The employee also met in a more formal way with community groups (residential and service oriented). In addition, she lived for a week in a Granville Street hotel and during that week wandered the streets at various times of the day and night, ate in the local beaneries, hung out with the people, and listened to what they had to say about a gathering place in their area.

The least successful approach to the folks of Downtown South was made by their kin at the Carnegie Centre. An April 2 event was advertised up and down Granville, and Carnegie staff, board, and volunteers set up an Open House at 401 Main. The theatre boasted tables with information about setting up a board, how a volunteer program works, Library and Learning Centre displays, samples of cross-cultural programming (complete with smouldering sweet grass, beadwork in process, international music), and – of course – bottomless pots and trays of Carnegie coffee and cookies. The hosts had a terrific time. Unfortunately, not a soul turned up from Downtown South.

The information gathering is not complete. The voice of market renters is yet to be recorded and native people have made no statement. A storefront needs to be set up to encourage further community input, but even at this point there is no shortage of opinions about what a community centre in Downtown South might look like.

Some Opinions

Street Kids: One street kid, let's call her Lilly, left northern Ontario three years ago at the age of fourteen, and has lived in several of Canada's large cities. Despite the wandering, she is about to graduate from high school, possible, she says, because Vancouver offers "the best" services to street youth, and workers here eased her back into an alternate school.

Lilly has spent some of the past three years squatting. She has a cat and the first day we met she had no money. The honorarium I gave paid first for cat food, then for cigarettes, and then for food for herself.

Lilly is a healthy looking teenager, dressed in leather and studs, with hair of many lengths and many colours (red, blue, green, orange, brown). She and her friends panhandle on Granville and she says they won't use needles or sell their bodies or mug anyone – not, that is, unless they're really hungry. Food is a big issue, and cigarettes and drugs help when a ravenous kid (with no place to sleep) wanders the strip through the night. Lilly says she can tell at this stage who on the street will and won't make it. She says she will, and she will likely end up working with kids like herself. In her experience, the best street workers are the ones who have been there themselves.

Lilly says she and the youngsters who look like her are dehumanized by meatheads, her name for Granville pedestrians, probably businessmen, wearing suits. The kids respond positively to folks who acknowledge a panhandling request but turn it down. What they hate is the meathead who looks through them, who doesn't see them. I witnessed that, sitting with Lilly on the steps of the Art Gallery. A TV news camera crew approached everyone on the steps – behind us, in front of us, to either side of us. In Lilly's company, she and the writer both became invisible. Lilly says she used to be hurt by that rejection. Now she's angered by it and butts up against it.

Lilly and some of her friends have visited Carnegie, but don't find it very friendly. They'd rather have a centre in the Granville area. Their dream facility would include storage space, showers, and a laundromat – all the things that kids on the move don't have easy access to. Lilly says scabies went up and down the strip last year and no one really knew how to get rid of it; some of the cleaning and health services provided by the Evelyne Saller Centre are needed downtown. The wish list of the street kids includes a centre as a safe place, with no booze or drugs allowed. The young people want a reading room with newspapers and referral to local services. They'd like a meeting room, free phones, and bus tickets. They like the sound of Carnegie's music program, and sometimes they'd like to watch movies or videos, play pool and cards, or just hang out doing nothing. A gym with a punching bag would be well used. And food, don't forget food. Good food. Real food. Cheap food. Lilly thinks the kids could be referred to a volunteer kitchen program by the service agencies and she thinks they would help prepare and serve food in exchange for meals, just the way volunteers do at Carnegie.

Lilly and her friends have a lot to offer in the development of a gathering place. But she'll be damned if she'll sit on a formal committee with a bunch of meatheads. For now her information will only flow in an informal way through personal contact.

Youth service workers downtown also support the concept of a gathering place. But in addition to the things the kids listed, they add a literacy program, a native worker to deal specifically with the young native men involved in the sex trade, the program flexibility to provide a sewing program for "drag queens" making dresses, one-to-one counselling, food, affordable housing, and a place to crash during the day. But they say life in the centre shouldn't be made too comfortable, because no one wants a kid to get stuck there.

DERA: A DERA gathering place committee has met weekly to discuss their wish list. They've also visited possible sites downtown and toured Carnegie to see what's offered there. The group has put together and presented to this writer their comprehensive plan to meet community needs. [DERA's recommendations include: a regulation-size gym floor, a Universal Gym and weight room, showers, lockers, and a sauna, a library and reading room, games rooms/lounge space, rec room, auditorium, seminar rooms, first aid, a kitchen, and offices.]

As their terms of reference, the committee states its purpose is to "acquire property, permits, and funding, to establish a Downtown South community centre. The group is in the process of being incorporated under the Societies Act. The association will elect a Board of Directors, of which a majority will be long-term residents of the Downtown South to ensure that the community centre becomes a facility for existing residents."

Certainly, DERA played a significant role in the establishment of the Carnegie Centre, and the Carnegie Community Centre Association is incorporated under the Societies Act for the purpose of fundraising and distribution of official income tax receipts. At this stage in Carnegie's life though, DERA plays no role in the running of the centre. Carnegie has the singular position of being a City of Vancouver facility with city staff and city funds plus an elected independent community board which feels free to tackle neighbourhood issues, including those critical of the city. The advantage of this unique situation must not be underestimated.

Other Options

Granville Street merchants are very receptive to the prospect of a gathering place, and those contacted so far have been helpful (posting notices) and respectful when speaking of the potential patrons. Only one businessman, a real estate agent, tossed off a remark about low life.

One politician thinks the gathering place should target only the disadvantaged because market renters have the West End Community Centre at one end and the Round House at the other. In addition, the neighbourhood offers several fitness centres and at least one apartment offers a club membership as part of the tenancy.

Another politician encouraged this writer to think big, to look for a square block which could include the gathering place, green space, social housing, and a food co-op.

Serious consideration must be given to the issue of food shopping in the downtown area. On Granville itself, the tiny stores have a limited selection and high prices. One woman on social assistance uses her bus pass to travel to Metrotown because things cost so much less. The community worker from Jubilee Housing has drafted a proposal for a food co-op/store to be tried out for the New Continental.

Where?

Some think it would be appropriate to convert a heritage-type building for use, as at Carnegie. Others think a vacant lot should be selected and a facility built according to need. (There's no doubt that Carnegie has experienced certain stresses trying to squeeze all possible uses into limited available space.) There may also be possibilities within city-owned properties in the area. The expertise of the Housing and Properties Department will be required before any suggestions can be brought forth.

What Now?

The Housing and Properties Department is currently investigating possible sites for a modest store-front location.

A site on Granville, with 1200 square feet, can be used for the collecting of information about the gathering place and for the sharing of information by folks from Carnegie and elsewhere. The street kids (and their staff supervisor) may use the space to work on their newsletter. Health counselling, impact development committee meetings, and other community uses will be encouraged so that the city space impacts on the neighbourhood.

A young architectural student recently offered me his vision of the gathering place as "a bridge between the people who are in Downtown South now and those who will be there in the future." I wonder.

> Child poverty will remain a serious problem in Canada in the 1990s unless we undertake a comprehensive strategy to fight it. This policy paper takes the position that labour market-related policies must play a crucial role in that strategy. Where possible, it is preferable to raise the incomes of the poor through labour market-related policies and programs rather than through non-labour market-related transfers [i.e. welfare payments].
>
> *Employment & Labour Market Policy*

Epilogue

I have been thinking about who I should dedicate this book to. I started to think about all the children that are at this moment suffering hunger, abuse, unloved, unwanted . . . My mind as usual flips to my childhood. Tears start to wobble my eyes. My nose runs, sadness overwhelms me.

The damage that can't be repaired leaves me weary. I know I wasn't loved or wanted as a child, and the child in me says there must be something wrong with me to be so unloved.

I struggle with the reality, which is that I have children, grandchildren, and friends that love me dearly. I have daughters-in-law, sons-in-law that love me too. However, this deep pain of childhood creeps in, in what should be my happiest moments. There is a scar there, scars don't go away. They are the results of wounds, emotional wounds that are deep.

I know I have great difficulty loving myself. Somehow that just isn't enough, me loving me. I have the answer, but not the process for solving the question. I know without a doubt there are millions of adults who feel this way too . . . I start to censor my thoughts with a "stop complaining." I think of the Serenity Prayer: "God give me the serenity to accept the things I cannot change . . . "

As a child, "God" was a monster who was watching me all the time and allowed bad things to happen to me. As an adult "He," the great "He," made me feel guilty for hating my oppressors.

I know there is a Higher Spirit. I know that my Higher Spirit loves me. I just struggle with a word to name it. The word "God" is definitely out. Too many children have suffered in the name of God, by adults using the God word to manipulate and control and abuse.

This late October the sky is a multitude of shades of grey, the seagulls are complaining with loud squeals and squawks. This is the last I will write about Sheila for this book. I'm sorry I can't say I love me. I love me. I just know that I need to.

❖

A special thank you to:

End Legislated Poverty.

New Star (Audrey, my editor; Rolf, my publisher; Karen, my publicist).

All the children and all the people who are in this book, thank you, without you there wouldn't be a book.

The National Anti-Poverty Organization (especially Rosemary Spendlove).

The Ministry of Labour, provincial and federal.

Family Advancement Program staff.

Carnegie, DERA, DEYAS, Crabtree, SPARC.

Gordon Neighbourhood House.

Communications Division of the Ministry of Social Services.

Penny Parry.

The Ombudsperson in Victoria.

Friends and family, for their encouragement.

VanCity: their prize money helped me buy some material I needed for this book.

A special thanks to Patty, she really inspired me.

Appendix I: Grandma Baxter Stories

Illustrations by C.J.

The librarian who works with children and youth at the Vancouver Public Library asked me to do reading at the library. She said she was going to invite some students from a school in a different area of the city to hear me read. She, like me, felt that children should be taught the reasons for poverty. She suggested that I write some children's stories about poverty, for children, and put them in the back of this book, so here they are. This is my idea of the kind of poverty curriculum that should be taught in school, giving children a healthy, non-judgmental classroom.

❖

Hi there.
My name is Grandma Baxter. I have eight grandchildren.
My grandchildren like me to tell them stories.
I would like to share some with you.
If you are feeling really happy, tell someone.
If you are feeling really sad, tell someone.
Do you go to school?
Do you go to pre-school?
Do you go to daycare?
Do you stay home?
I believe everyone is special in their own way.
I believe that you are a very fine person indeed.
Do you feel that you are special?

School and Kirk

Kirk is five years old. It is his first day in school.

He is a little scared.

Kirk has a brother and a sister. They are too young to go to school.

Sometimes Kirk's family has to go to the food bank for food.

A food bank is where people who have very little money can get food.

Kirk's family receives money from the government. This money is sometimes called welfare.

Welfare is for people who can't work for one reason or another.

Kirk's parent is sometimes very tired, because it is hard work trying to make the little bit of money go so far.

Kirk's family loves him very much. He is a fine boy.

Kirk and his family often go without things that families who have money can buy.

Kirk's teacher is very wise. She makes sure that the children she teaches understand what being poor means. Being poor or rich has nothing to do with who a child is. A child is a child. That's all.

What does being poor mean? What is welfare? What is a food bank?

Do you agree that Kirk is a fine child?

❖

School and Anna May

Anna May is feeling sad. Anna May is starting a new school today. Anna May is nine years old.

Anna May lives in a foster home. She has foster parents.

Anna May's family can not take care of her.

Anna May is feeling lonely. She has a new home and a new school. Foster homes are for children who for one reason or another can't stay at home. Children who are in foster care have a social worker who helps choose the right foster parents. Some children go back to their own home after the problems have been worked out.

Anna May needs to be treated with lots of kindness.

She also needs new friends, so be friendly to her, play with her. Make her welcome and then she will smile.

Anna May is a fine person.

Anna May's teacher is very wise and she teaches the children in her class that all children are equal.

What is foster care? What is a social worker?

How would you feel if you were in a foster home and in a new school?

Kirk

Kirk is nine years old now. His brother is in Grade 1 and his little sister goes to daycare.

Kirk's parent has a job. That means Kirk has to help quite a bit at home. Kirk had hoped that now his family was not on welfare, he could be happier.

Kirk's parent works all day, then picks up Kirk's sister from daycare and his younger brother from after-school care. They go home and his parent makes supper, does the laundry, bathes the children.

Kirk's parent is so tired. There is just so much to do. His parent told him that money still doesn't go very far, because minimum wage is so low.

Kirk is feeling sad. His parent is even more tired and there is so little money. He thinks as soon as he can he will quit school and get a job.

His parent told him that that is not wise, because if he quits school he will get a job that pays very little. He must stay in school.

Kirk's teacher is very wise. He teaches his class about poverty and the minimum wage. The class discusses it.

Kirk feels a little less sad, but it hasn't solved his family's problems.

What does it feel like to be poor? Is it a child's fault if his family is poor?

Do you know what minimum wage is?

Can you study well if you feel sad?

❖

Marty

It is Marty's first day in school.

He misses his mother.

Marty looks at the other children in his class.

Many of the

children have different-coloured skin, different-coloured eyes, and different-coloured hair. Marty is different too.

Marty smiles at the child next to him and the child smiles back.

Marty has learned at home that every child is special and wonderful. He remembers that and feels very happy.

Marty's teacher is very wise. She treats each child as a very special person.

Do you think all children are special?

Are you special?

Is it alright to be different?

Do you feel different sometimes?

❖

Eloise

Eloise is eight years old. She is feeling sad and scared.

The people in her family are refugees. A refugee is someone who has to leave her country because she is in great danger.

Eloise does not speak English very well.

Eloise needs to make new friends.

The children in her class treat her very well.

Eloise is a very fine person.

Eloise's teacher is very wise. She explains to her class about poverty and about people who are refugees.

Do you know what not having very much money means?

How do you think a child who is a refugee feels?

What do you think would make her feel better?

❖

Kim and school

Kim is seven years old.

Kim comes to school in a wheelchair.

Kim has a special assistant to help her in school.

Kim in unable to walk.

Kim wants to talk with children in her class.

Kim wants to play too.

Kim is a very fine child, just like any other child.

She wants to make friends.

How do you think you would feel if you couldn't walk?

How would you like other children to treat you if you were in a wheelchair?

Some children have problems speaking . . . hearing . . . thinking . . . all kinds of problems. But they too like to learn and make friends.

How would like to be treated if you had a problem?

Appendix II: Resources

Most of the following list is drawn from Campaign 2000's contact list of groups fighting child poverty across Canada. I have also included organizations that I've mentioned in the book.

Penelope Rowe
Community Services Council
Virginia Park Plaza, Ste. 101, 2nd Flr.
Newfoundland Dr.
St. John's, NF A1A 3E9
709-753-9860

Elaine Perkins
Fredericton Anti-Poverty Org.
120 King St.
Fredericton, NB E3B 1C9
506-458-9102

June Weir
Caring About People in Poverty
60 Ellenvale Ave.
Dartmouth, NS B2W 2W5
902-464-2380

Paul O'Hara
North End Community Clinic
2165 Gottigen St.
Halifax, NS B3K 3B5
902-420-0303

Barbara Blouin
Nova Scotia Coalition for Children & Youth
6940 Tupper Grove
Halifax, NS B3H 2M6
902-429-2235

Philip Smith
Child Poverty PEI: Campaign 2000
c/o Philip Smith
Dept. of Psychology
University of PEI
Charlottetown, PEI C1A 4P3
903-566-0422

Nikki Aumond
Montreal YMCA
1441 Drummond Ave.
Montreal, PQ H3G 1W3
514-849-5331

Elaine Eastman
Halton Social Planning Council
760 Brant St., Ste. 406B
Burlington, ON L7R 4B7
416-632-1975

Wendell Fields
Hamilton Against Poverty
25 Hughson Street S., Ste. 506
Hamilton, ON L8N 2A5
416-529-7327

Sharon Laffrenier
Hamilton Against Poverty
118 Brucedale E.
Hamilton, ON L9A 1N4
416-575-9127

Don Jaffray
Hamilton-Wentworth Child Poverty Forum
c/o Social Planning and Research Council
155 James St. S., Ste. 601
Hamilton, ON L8P 3A4
416-522-1148

Susan Eagle
Southwestern Ontario Child Poverty Action Group
Box 1578, Stn. A
London, ON N6A 5M3
519-657-8720

Sharon Douglas
Social Planning Council of Peel
977 Pantera Dr., Unit 8
Mississauga, ON L4W 2T4
416-629-3044

Colin Hughes
Children's Aid Society of Metro Toronto
180 Duncan Mill Rd., 2nd Flr.
North York, ON M3B 1Z6
416-924-4646

Patrick Johnston
Canadian Council on Social Development
55 Parkdale Ave.
Box 3505, Stn. C
Ottawa, ON K1Y 4G1
613-728-1865

Barbara Kilbride
Canadian Day Care Advocacy Assoc.
232 Chapel St.
Ottawa, ON K1N 7Z2
613-594-3196

Sylvia Haines
Canadian Housing and Renewal Assoc.
251 Laurier Ave. W., Ste. 304
Ottawa, ON K1P 5J6
613-594-3007

Carmelo Spiteri
Canadian Seniors for Social Responsibility
145 Spruce St., Ste. 202B
Ottawa, ON K1R 6P1
613-230-3316

Heather-Jane Robertson
Canadian Teachers' Federation
110 Argyle Ave.
Ottawa, ON K2P 1B4
613-232-1505

Canadian Youth Foundation
2211 Riverside Dr., Ste. 11
Ottawa, ON K1H 7X5
613-731-2733

Sandra Scarth
Child Welfare League
180 Argyle Ave., Ste. 312
Ottawa, ON K2P 1B7
613-235-4412

CEJY (Children*Enfants*Jeunesse*Youth)
55 Parkdale
Ottawa, ON K1Y 1E5
613-722-0133

Mel Gill
Children's Aid Society of Ottawa-Carleton
1370 Bank St.
Ottawa, ON K1H 7Y3
613-733-1600

Trevor Williams
Family Service Canada
55 Parkdale Ave.
Ottawa, ON K1Y 4G1
613-728-2463

Lynne Toupin
National Anti-Poverty Org.
256 King Edward Ave., Ste. 316
Ottawa, ON K1N 7M1
613-789-0141

National Council of Welfare
Jeanne Mance Building
Ottawa, ON K1A 0K9
613-957-2961

National Youth in Care Network
119 Murray St.
Ottawa, ON K1N 5M5
613-236-9289

Helen Saravanamuttoo
Ottawa-Carleton Child Poverty Action Group
949 Kingsmere Ave.
Ottawa, ON K1N 7M1
613-737-5115 ext. 333

Cindy Moriarty
Social Planning Council of Ottawa-Carleton
256 King Edward Ave.
Ottawa, ON K1N 7M1
613-236-3658

Noelle-Dominique Willems
YWCA of/du Canada
100 Argyle St.
Ottawa, ON K2P 1B4
613-594-3649

Adje van de Sande
Laurentian University
School of Social Work
Sudbury, ON P3E 2C6
705-675-1151 ext. 5066

Michael Cushing
Child Poverty Action 2000-Niagara
c/o Niagara Children's Services Committee
3550 Schmon Parkway
Thorold, ON L2V 4Y6
416-984-4033/1-800-461-3032

Brenda Reimer
Lakehead Social Planning Council
125 Syndicate Ave. S.
Thunder Bay, ON P7E 6H8
807-626-9650

Linda Nicholl
Peter Clutterbuck
Campaign 2000
c/o Social Planning Council of Metro Toronto
2 Carlton St., Ste. 1001
Toronto, ON M5B 1J3
416-351-0095

Barry Davidson
Canadian Assoc. of Food Banks
530 Lakeshore Blvd. W.
Toronto, ON M5V 1A5
416-777-9241

Ed Pennington
Canadian Mental Health Assoc.
2160 Yonge St., 3rd Flr.
Toronto, ON M4S 2Z3
416-484-7750

Rosemarie Popham
Child Poverty Action Group
c/o Family Service Assoc.
22 Wellesley St. E.
Toronto, ON M4Y 1G3
416-922-3126

Malcolm Shookner
Ontario Social Development Council
130 Spadina Ave., Ste. 402
Toronto, ON M5V 2L4
416-594-2351

Rev. David Pfrimmer
Interfaith Social Assistance Review Coalition
Waterloo-Lutheran Seminary
Waterloo, ON N2L 3C5
519-884-1970 ext. 2907

Diane Garvin
Children's Services Council (Durham) Inc.
1650 Dundas St. E.
Whitby, ON L1N 2K8
416-433-4100

Mary Medcalf
Legal Assistance of Windsor
85 Pitt St. E.
Windsor, ON N9A 2V3
519-256-7831

Maureen Kalloo
Social Planning Council of Winnipeg
412 McDermot Ave.
Winnipeg, MB R3A 0A9
204-943-2561

Lorelee Manning
Council on Social Development
2445-13 Ave., Rm. 330
Regina, SK S4P 0W1
306-565-8575

Avenue 15
938 15 Ave. SW
Calgary, AB T2R 0S3
403-244-4847

Alison Macdonald
Edmonton Social Planning Council
41-9912-106 St.
Edmonton, AB T5K 1C5
403-423-2031

Cecile Guay
Federated Anti-Poverty Group of B.C.
3-956 Cornwall Cres.
Dawson Creek, BC V1G 1N9
604-782-8484

Child Advocate
Vancouver City Hall
453 West 12 Ave.
Vancouver, BC V5Y 1V4
604-873-7011

Betty McPhee
Crabtree Corners
101 East Cordova
Vancouver, BC V6A 1K7
604-689-2808

John Turvey
Downtown Eastside Youth Activities Society
223 Main St.
Vancouver, BC V6A 2S7
604-685-6561

End Legislated Poverty
211-456 West Broadway
Vancouver, BC V5Y 1R3
604-879-1209

Family Advancement Program
1616 West 7 Ave.
Vancouver, BC V6J 1S5
604-731-4951

Maggie Duckett
Gordon House Youth Works
1237 Richards St.
Vancouver, BC V6B 3G4
604-687-8868

David Hay
Social Planning and Research Coun.
108-2182 West 12 Ave.
Vancouver, BC V6K 2N4
604-736-8118

Pat Chauncey
End Legislated Poverty
c/o Together Against Poverty Society
615-620 View St.
Victoria, BC V8W 1J6
604-383-8778

Bibliography

Axworthy, Chris. "Changing Course: An NDP Action Plan on Poverty." May 1992.

Baker, Maureen. "Canadian Youth in a Changing World." Library of Parliament, Research Branch, March 1989.

Baxter, Sheila. *No Way to Live: Poor Women Speak Out.* (Vancouver: New Star Books, 1988)

Baxter, Sheila. *Under the Viaduct: Homeless in Beautiful B.C.* (Vancouver: New Star Books, 1991)

British Columbia: Ministry of Social Services. *Liberating Our Children, Liberating Our Nations.* Report of the Aboriginal Committee, Community Panel, Family and Children's Services Legislation Review in B.C., October 1992.

British Columbia: Ministry of Social Services. *Making Changes: A Place to Start.* Report of the Community Panel, Family and Children's Services Legislation Review in B.C., October 1992.

British Columbia: Ministry of Social Services. "Protecting Our Children/Supporting Our Families: A Review of Child Protection Issues in British Columbia." January 1992.

British Columbia: Office of the Ombudsman. "Public Services to Children, Youth and Their Families in British Columbia: The Need for Integration." Public Report #22, November 1990.

British Columbia: Office of the Ombudsman. "Public Response to Request for Suggestions for Legislative Change to Family and Child Service Act." February 1991.

B.C. Government Employees Union. "Abandoned Teens: A Report on Government Services for Teenagers in B.C." October 1986.

B.C. Nutrition Council. "The Poor Still Can't Afford to Eat in B.C." Press release, March 4, 1992.

Bibliography

Canadian Council on Social Development. "Economic and Social Welfare for Families and Children." Newsletter #1, June 1992.

Canadian Teachers' Federation. "Children, Schools and Poverty." CEJY, 1992.

Castelle, Kay. "Children Have Rights too! A Primer on the UN Convention on the Rights of the Child." Defense for Children International-Canada (Anglophone), 1990.

"Child Poverty – Who Needs It?" Conference report sponsored by the New Brunswick Child Welfare Association, Moncton, NB, May 1991.

Child Poverty Action Group, Institute for the Prevention of Child Abuse, Ontario Association of Children's Aid Societies. "Poor People are Not the Problem . . . Poverty Is." 1990.

Clark, Gordon. "Lack of jobs plagues youth." Vancouver *Province*, October 21, 1992.

Clarke, Michelle. "Fighting Poverty Through Programs: Social and Health Programs for Canada's Poor Children and Youth." CEJY, 1992.

Cox, Bob. "Community is solution for youth crime." Vancouver *Sun*, October 24, 1992.

Craig, Ailsa. "Living and Learning in Poverty." *B.C. Teacher*, May/June 1987.

Doyle, Veronica. "Housing and Children in Canada." CEJY, November 1991.

Duckett, Maggie. "Gordon House Youth Works 1992-1993 Operating Proposal." Unpublished, January 1992.

End Legislated Poverty. "Brief to the B.C. Royal Commission on Education." March 1, 1988.

Flekkøy, Målfrid Grude. "Working for the Rights of Children: The Experience of the Norwegian Ombudsman for Children." UNICEF, n.d.

"Family forced to split after mother dies." Vancouver *Province*, August 5, 1992.

Gathia, Joseph. "Child Labour: A Question of Dignity." *Libertas* (International Centre for Human Rights and Democratic Development), Vol. 2, No. 4, October 1992.

"General Survey of the Reports Relating to Convention No. 138 and Recommendation No. 146 Concerning Minimum Age." International Labour Conference, 67th Session, 1981.

Goldberg, Michael. "Implications of the Federal Budget for Children and Child Care: A SPARC Discussion Paper." Unpublished paper from the Social Planning and Research Council of B.C., April 1992.

Government of Canada. "The Government Response to the Report of the Standing Committee on Health and Welfare, Social Affairs, Seniors and the Status of Women: Canada's Children: Investing in our Future." May 1992.

Government of Canada: Health and Welfare Canada. "Brighter Futures." May 1992.
Government of Canada: Health and Welfare Canada. "Children of Canada, Children of the World." Canada's National Paper for the World Summit for Children, 1990
Government of Canada: House of Commons. "Canada's Children: Investing in our Future. Report of the Standing Committee on Health and Welfare, Social Affairs, Seniors and the Status of Women (Sub-Committee on Poverty)." December 1991.
Government of Canada: Senate. "Child Poverty and Adult Social Problems: Interim Report of the Standing Senate Committee on Social Affairs, Science and Technology." December 1989.
Government of Canada: Senate. "Children in Poverty: Toward a Better Future." Standing Senate Committee of Social Affairs, Science and Technology, January 1991.
Hilt, Caroline and Sarah Hopper. "Making the Difference!" Canadian Youth Foundation, April 1989.
Hopper, Sarah. "Violence in Canadian Society: A Youth Concern." *Youth Policy Today*, Vol. 3, No. 2, Summer 1988.
Hossie, Linda. "Battling the bare bones of child poverty: UNICEF Reports." *Globe and Mail*, December 18, 1992.
"Income and the Labour Market." *Youth Policy Today*, Vol. 3, No. 4, Winter 1989.
Kane, Michael. "Taxing Children." Vancouver *Sun*, December 7, 1992.
Lynn, John. "The Children of Divorce." *B.C. Council for the Family Newsletter*, Vol. 12, No. 1, Spring 1990.
MacQueen, Ken. "Fight crime with day care." Vancouver *Sun*, March 5, 1993.
Marcotte, Linda. "Child Poverty: Making the Connections." Unpublished paper, September 22, 1992.
Michaud, Margaret A. *Dead End: Homeless Teenagers, A Multi-Service Approach*. (Calgary: Detselig Enterprises, 1988)
Mickleburgh, Rod. "Silver threads threaten to strangle the system." *Globe and Mail*, April 27, 1992.
Munro, Harold. "Turning it around." Vancouver *Sun*, October 24, 1992.
National Anti-Poverty Organization. "Written Submission to the Legislative Committee on Bill C-80." Unpublished paper, July 16, 1992.
National Council of Welfare. "Poor Kids: A Report by the National Council of Welfare on Children in Poverty in Canada." March 1975.
National Council of Welfare. "Welfare Incomes 1990." Autumn 1991.
National Council of Welfare. "Funding Health and Higher Education: Danger Looming." 1991.
National Council of Welfare. "The Canada Assistance Plan: No Time for Cuts." Winter 1991.

National Council of Welfare. "Welfare Incomes 1991." Summer 1992.

National Council of Welfare. "Welfare Reform." Summer 1992.

National Council of Welfare. "The 1992 Budget and Child Benefits." Autumn 1992.

National Youth in Care Network. "General Overview of the National Youth in Care Network." Unpublished paper, 1991.

"NDP job and training changes will help people on welfare a bit." *End Legislated Poverty Newsletter*, October 1992.

Parry, Penny. "Thoughts on Advocacy." Unpublished paper, 24 September 1992.

Parton, Nicole. "Hockey star Lowe ordered to pay potential $600,000 child support." Vancouver *Sun*, December 8, 1992.

Posterski, Donald and Reginald Bibby. "Canada's Youth: Ready for Today. A Comprehensive Survey of 15-24 Year Olds." Canadian Youth Foundation, n.d.

Radford, Joyce L., Alan J.C. King, Wendy K. Warren. *Street Youth & AIDS*. Social Program Evaluation Group, Queen's University, 1989. (Available from Federal Centre for AIDS, Health Protection Branch, Health and Welfare Canada, 301 Elgin Street, Ottawa, Ontario K1A 0L2)

Rees, Ann. "Hard Times Taking Toll." Vancouver *Province*, January 24, 1993.

Rickard, D'Arcy. "A nightmare is erased by a loving place." *Education Leader* (B.C. School Trustees Association), Vol. 5, No. 19, November 6, 1992.

Ross, Lia. "Canada's Youth." Statistics Canada Catalogue 98-124, September 1989.

Ryan, Thomas J. editor. *Poverty and the Child: A Canadian Study*. (Toronto: McGraw-Hill Ryerson Ltd., 1972)

Ryerse, Catherine. *Thursday's Child: Child Poverty in Canada: A Review of the Effects of Poverty on Children*. National Youth in Care Network, 1990.

Sarti, Robert. "A place to call her own." Vancouver *Sun*, November 10, 1992.

Sarti, Robert. "Proposed youth housing in Gastown draws fire." Vancouver *Sun*, November 12, 1992.

Schwartz, Susan. "An ounce of Prevention." Montreal *Gazette*, October 19, 1992.

Sinclair, Donna. "What it's like to have little." *United Church Observer*, March 1992.

Social Planning Council of Ottawa-Carleton, Income and Employment Forum. "Employment and Labour Market Policy." CEJY, 1992.

Street Children: A Growing Urban Tragedy. Report for the Independent Commission on International Humanitarian Issues. (London: Weidenfeld & Nicolson, 1986).

Sunter, Deborah. "Juggling school and work." *Perspectives* (Statistics Canada), Spring 1992.

Swanson, Jean. "Tory Government Sneaks in the Big Business Version of the Guaranteed Annual Income." *NAPO News,* No. 37, Summer 1992.

"Tough Times: The Situation of Homeless Youth" *Youth Policy Today,* Vol. 2, No. 2, 1987.

"Toward a perfect world." Kids Help Phone supplement in *Globe and Mail,* May 1, 1992.

"Two million kids at work in hidden army" *The New Review #9,* April/May 1991.

Usinger, Mike. "Equal Education Essential." Vancouver *Courier,* March 8, 1992.

Vancouver: Social Planning Department. "Children and Youth at Risk: Towards a Mental Health Plan for Metropolitan Vancouver." Children and Youth at Risk Steering Committee, November 1991.

Vancouver: Social Planning Department. "Downtown South Implementation Program: Interim Report." July 21, 1992.

von Hauff, Donna. "Young First-Time Workers." *Occupational Health & Safety Magazine,* Autumn 1989.

Webber, Marlene. *Street Kids: The Tragedy of Canada's Runaways.* (Toronto: University of Toronto Press, 1991).

Wong, Chung. "Wheelchair panhandler hands over to the kids." Vancouver *Province,* August 23, 1992.

York, Geoffrey. "Coalition stresses plight of poor children." *Globe and Mail,* November 22, 1991.

Index